Six Secessional Signs

Why America Must Come Apart

Trent W. Ling

ISBN: 0615682464
ISBN-13: 978-0615682464

DEDICATION

For freedom-loving people everywhere who would and will dare to work hard and dream big for the benefit and enrichment of others

ON THE COVER

A 2008 aerial view of Alaska's massive Mount McKinley range demonstrates the strata of possibilities in a free America. Strangely and immorally, 2013 America resembles what would be an intentional flattening and repackaging of these potentials.

CONTENTS

ACKNOWLEDGMENTS

To the family for enduring this ill-timed albatross.
To David for his keen eye and bold suggestions.
To readers who have somehow not yet given up on liberty.

INTRODUCTION

Tragically, the United States has expired. History. Kaput. Toast. It was an incredible run, but it has come to a crashing conclusion. Short of indispensible but unpalatable legislative rollbacks in this deeply divided country, no trajectory of survival, let alone of victory, can again be attained. The nature of the political and social stalemates leaves the clocks ticking while the nation's institutions remain paralyzed. Social Security and Medicare head for insolvency while the current government continues to out-borrow and over-spend its wildest dreams. Those who care about self-determination—admittedly a distinct minority worldwide—can scarcely find viable and prosperous routes through the national hodgepodge while simultaneously saddled with carrying the dead weight of an indifferent or downright resistant majority. Those at ease with this gasping situation exhibit zero regard for liberty—theirs or anybody else's.

Many competing preambles and imperatives jostle for primacy in this straightforward assessment of America in 2013. Frustratingly, no immediate salve can be identified or heeded quickly enough to deliver wholly this downwardly spiraling nation of such strategic and historic prominence. Nonetheless, this missive—largely aimed against fear and stupidity, and designed for a day's reading and a lifetime of digestion at the nominal cost of a combo meal—timely arrives to provide a desperately needed conversational shift for appalled freedom-loving Americans. Sign by sign, a landscape of issues, ideas, and examples are originally presented and sensibly reconciled.

As the sinking of the *Lusitania* precipitated entry of the United States into World War I, the educational light from American "secession talk" will eventually prompt free peoples' departure from the suicidal United States. Those even remotely interested in self-determination will recognize that status quo alternatives to secession offer nothing more than inexorable, wholesale collapse.

Humans, endowed by God and not fundamentally subject to government evaluation or usury, need not ever accede to any false presidential choices offering no candidate who can or could ever deliver in the face of present challenges and tasks. Save for the rousing rhetoric and stirringly hopeful words and ideas of 2012 GOP presidential primary candidate Newt Gingrich, nobody has proffered any notion or idea that even begins to address the size and scope of America's intractably mounting problems. Resounding proof of this came post-election in 2012 when both Democrats and Republicans quickly unified to ridicule and dissuade embryonic petitions for secession filed by citizens on behalf of each of the 50 states. In a damaging parallel, these flaky politicians in an impromptu group hug against secession unwittingly find themselves on the very wrong side of Scriptural history. Back in Biblical times, enemies

King Herod and Governor Pilate suddenly became friends over their mutually greater hatred of Jesus Christ. Today, warring political parties similarly become pals in joint disdain for the notion that someone somewhere might somehow break away to prosperity and happiness.

Liberal Democrats in America 2013 would have been laughed out of the Constitutional Convention had they proffered their shallow ideas to the nation's founders in 1787. So far afield have Blue-State enthusiasts ("Blues") gone that they have become simply unrecognizable to their counterpart proponents of Red States ("Reds"). As Americans scrambled, contemplated, and argued for a better course for the Union 226 years ago, citizens across the vast plains must rouse similarly today. By revisiting the Republic's founding and wholly bypassing today's loudmouths—who would have received no ear back then, anyway—those loyal to founding principles may yet salvage most of what once stood as the crown jewel of nations.

Reds must frame and press an overdue state-by-state introspection precipitating peaceful secession from the United States. At first unthinkable, then intriguing, next palatable, eventually necessary, and finally understood as brilliant, secession provides the lone remaining hope for American idealism and its historically delivered realism. While supposedly patriotic adults enjoy sharing with school children soaring quotes of national founders (e.g., Patrick Henry's, "Give me liberty or give me death"), those same adults seem loath to mouth such things themselves, let alone believe them, enjoy them, or effectuate them in their day.

Should any government official arise one day and shock the world by acknowledging that Red-State secession is a right and a necessity to preserve any liberty for those on "American" soil, then good for them. But with or without their understanding, allowance, or support, the Red States and their backers will ultimately secede from the Blue nonsense.

The Scriptures, the American Declaration of Independence ("Declaration"), and the United States Constitution ("Constitution") militate in unison toward Red-State secession from "America." Sprinkled throughout this work, the expressions, purposes, and ideals of these three documents show their muscle and wisdom that birthed America. Over time, however, America's shunning of these instruments has completely unwound America. Consider these timeless and urgent words from the Declaration:

> "We hold these truths to be self-evident, that all men are created equal, that they are endowed by their Creator with certain unalienable Rights, that among these are Life, Liberty and the pursuit of Happiness. That to secure these rights, Governments are instituted among Men, deriving their just powers from the consent of the governed, That whenever any Form of Government becomes destructive of these ends, it is the Right of the People to alter or to abolish it, and to institute new Government, laying its foundation on such principles and organizing its powers in such form, as to them shall seem most likely to effect their Safety and Happiness."

Surely, those who would object to the right and

prerogative of Red States to secede from the United States must also object to the original spirit, yearning, and plain language of this founding Declaration. For their parts, the Scriptures have advised that freedom should be gained if possible (1 Corinthians 7:21), and the Constitution promised that no federal government would overreach the states or the people (10th Amendment). The three most relevant documents in American lives still take the side of freedom and the side of those who would dare to long for and go for liberty, not only for themselves but also for those who would follow.

Purely Observational

Ironically, despite its edge, this essay sets out solely to share noticeable, understandable, truthful, and actionable observations. It does not advocate or push any particular course of action beyond acknowledging and proclaiming the truth and its inevitabilities. Educational at its core, this writing simply instigates sober and vigorous discussion regarding several long-ignored 800-pound gorillas. Within limited space, significant efforts attempt to shift the national conversation, flash warning signs to all, and provide a walkway through endless storms. What readers, leaders, and voters will do with the honesty and truth unveiled herein remains an open and lingering question for the days, months, years, and generations ahead.

Nobody should ever hide his head in the sand, and nobody should shrink back from stating the truth. God has built and displayed an incredible and glorifying array of people, places, and things worthy of observation and comment. For the benefit of the attentive, right and rich observations add heft, flavor, and color to life. Accordingly, Jesus routinely shared passing observations with keen insight and bountiful understanding. These extras from the Christ added greatly to what would otherwise have been an overly legalistic and dry Bible. In the political and governmental arena, for example, Jesus proved to be no shrinking violet as the Bible recounts: "At that time some Pharisees came to Jesus and said to him, 'Leave this place and go somewhere else. Herod wants to kill you.' He replied, 'Go tell that fox…'" (Luke 13:31-32). Obviously, the ever-watchful Jesus was well aware of King Herod, his ways, and his policies. As an observational matter, Jesus shared some truths about it. Jesus did not forsake his one-fold, heavenly mission to win the world by supplanting them with any earthly efforts to remove Herod from office. Rather, Jesus shared the depth of what he noticed to the benefit and enrichment of all. Across the landscapes of life, Jesus so gave. He offered his two cents on pain, loss, and heartache, along with his take on joy, gain, and hope. He paid attention, reached right conclusions, and offered them for the benefit of the interested. He knew and spoke freely of casts of characters, human history, and human hearts. He spoke with a depth and a breadth to be emulated by his true disciples, as could be read in the later works and words of John, Peter, and Paul. The life behind this book similarly strives herein to offer a bevy of truthful and enriching observations.

This essay has not at all been birthed, built, or crafted on the basis of any political partiality or philosophical favoritism, and no hate or animus resides within these pages. Rather, tough love and fierce loyalty abound for all. Purely observational, this work brandishes a series of sober offerings amidst a struggling world rattled by hysterical, tyrannical, and off-putting developments. May those with eyes and ears emerge from such chaos and join or rejoin the land of the living. The convictions posited herein maintain their footing from their inherent and undeniable rightness, and they are not subject to rejection or scorn on the basis of their understandability or likability. An abiding affinity for soaring ideals drives this writing, its horizons, admonitions, and conclusions. No doubt, many will disparage these words, distort this message, rail against the messenger, and contrarily insist that Americans plunge over the falls rather than escape the insanity of man-made hazards. So, turning a volitionally deaf ear to the grumblers and fixing a laser focus toward illuminating timeless truths, this writer opens a door to citizens and their states wishing *today* to get on with the original idea of America rather than awaiting America's inevitable asphyxiation and burial *tomorrow*.

This stark treatment of a handful of issues springs wholly from love of liberty and of similar higher ideals befitting humanity. This is not a rant for or against group, class, race, politics, religion, or education. Rather, this offering promotes individual liberty for all. Though Blue minds will invariably and conveniently forget or ignore this fact, it remains provably true. Only within this context can this work be understood, embraced, and digested. Those purposely or negligently forgetful of this will ruefully suffer the consequences and return to the diminutive existences, which their pining and voting have long foreshadowed.

Finally, and perhaps most importantly, this author readily and joyfully concedes that President Barack Obama, the Blues, and everyone else for that matter, are far better people than he. Far from "holier than thou," this writer remains convinced that though God shows him things and though God has made him more than he is and has delivered him from himself, he is in his natural self the worst of sinners. Never believe for a moment that this scribe has secured a vantage point looking down upon anybody. Deep in the trenches where he dwells, nothing could ever be further from the truth.

Why Secession?

Americans' forthcoming discussion of secession will enjoy rightful cover from First Amendment protections thus: "Congress shall make no law… abridging the freedom of speech… or the right of the people peaceably to assemble, and to petition the Government for a redress of grievances." Despite the temptation, no interference with secessional talk, debate, or assembly can be constitutionally had against Americans. Strangely, secession seems taboo and anathema in the United States, purportedly the freest of locales, but provides ready and immediate relief in all other regions of the world, especially in this present day.

Secession will hasten restoration and effectuation of the wisdom of the 10th Amendment: "The powers not delegated to the United States by the Constitution, nor prohibited by it to the States, are reserved to the States respectively, or to the people." States will again emerge as the geo-political entity of consequence, while the dizzying maze of the bloated federal bureaucracy will do whatever it does only to those sadly still tolerant of it. Through overreach in the federal courts, suffocating regulation from the White House, and carrot-and-stick relations from Congress, states' rights have been whittled down to mere afterthoughts. Only the headaches of governing remain to the states without any of the constitutionally promised elbowroom. The feds have taken the money and the power out of the states despite prohibitions against it. Generations of Americans have stood idly by largely because there always seemed to be enough to go around. But times have finally changed. Secession becomes necessary not as a preference or first resort or even as a fine idea, but as a matter of survival and in response to the final faint trumpet call of independence.

Far from a stretch or a move of desperation, secession has taken place peacefully and successfully across the globe for centuries and most notably over the past 25 years. Even dirt-poor and war-torn nations have emerged from the ashes by way of secession. How much better should Idaho and Utah have it? Nations arising from the iron-fisted and oppressive Soviet Union have made it. Why cannot Oklahoma do it? Even the world's most impoverished nations in Africa make it. Why not the Dakotas?

In Canada, Quebec often considers its own independence and secession. In America, territories like Puerto Rico seem empowered to decide for themselves whether to be or not to be American states. Should Alaska be denied the same prerogatives as Puerto Rico? On what philosophically durable grounds?

Why may Arizona and Texas not control their own borders with Mexico? Why must they suffer illegal immigration, border skirmishes, and drug, gang, and gun violence while the feds remain afraid to take a stand? Secession remains the only judicious option since the feds and the political parties have permanently embraced weakness and hand wringing because these seem to make for winning campaign strategies despite the disproportionate cost to the people of Arizona and Texas.

A recent effort in California sought to carve out and create a 51st state within the Golden State. Despite the brilliance of the idea, born of desperation in a bankruptcy-bound, deep-blue state, Article 4 Section 3 of the U.S. Constitution specifically prohibits the notion. In addition, nothing but the typically dissatisfied guffaw from the Blues greeted the idea. This noise need never again be tolerated after Reds leave the Union.

In 2013, secession can be undertaken responsibly, smartly, and transparently. With economic conditions in America suffering their worst trajectories in existing lifetimes, seceding states and their resident citizens must act expeditiously now that the writing on the wall seems to be of permanent ink. In this, President Obama will certainly mutter a series of illogical words written by others and purporting to express his opposition to secession. A Republican president would also most assuredly oppose secession (but likely only because opposition seems the politically correct thing to do for those who wish to man today's steering wheels). Whether either Obama now or Hillary Clinton in the next term would attempt to war against and/or nuke seceding states remains an open question for each to answer. Regardless of the tendencies of any commander-in-chief, true patriots simply cannot any longer tolerate this slow-motion shipwreck of a nation and its foggy people. End-game levels have long been reached. Whatever the failed office of the president chooses to do can hardly interest anyone with serious ideals and notions. The time for the president to weigh in has long passed. Perhaps Obama and/or Hillary would coldly butcher their own people like Russia's Stalin. Perhaps they would accommodate the break-up of the United States like Russia's Gorbachev managed the dissolution of the Soviet Union. Either way, the people must push forward and care little what the president decides to do because the luxury of paying him any more attention has expired.

Texas Governor Rick Perry caught some flack a few years back for suggesting that Texas might secede should Washington remain Washington (i.e., take, gobble, tax, spend). And during his ill-fated 2012 presidential primary campaign, Perry championed states' rights and the 10th Amendment at every turn. His public statements, Texas's Lone Star attitude, California's 51st-state initiative, and every syllable from President Obama being the latest, greatest silliness make ripe the idea of state secession while decent prospects of near-term success still obtain.

Yet, it has been shocking how conservatives, right-wingers, Republicans, and Tea Party backers have only messed around with notions aiming so far short of secession. They speak and warn of fiscal cliffs and wrong paths and backward ideologies, but they pussyfoot around as if this government, short of a thorough do-over hastened by mass Red-State exodus, can somehow be bandaged together enough to limp to any meaningful finish line. Crazy!

Fortunately for the genuine Reds, President Obama's broken-record existence keeps the same frustrations and fuels on the fire to give secession an inevitable hearing on the merits. Obama tends to the country as if it were some backwoods, hand-to-mouth state where primal solutions and ambitions were somehow expected to enthrall, satisfy, or appease scores of millions who have forever tasted and dreamed of better things. Confused by these sensibly recalcitrant citizens, Obama routinely lampoons them as selfish "fat cats" or people who do not pay their "fair share." Never smart enough, learned enough, or personally experienced enough, Obama still cannot see that his ultra-low-bar standards for living only satisfy him and his knee-jerk supporters. He seems destined forever to be confounded by the superior liberty for which his opponents are fully prepared to fight and die (as they have done throughout human history). Those emancipated in heart and mind have zero interest in living lives in the dirt or subject to horizons of the common wildebeest marked simply by mindless, dreamless grazing. The excruciatingly irreconcilable situation has reached its breaking point. Either Obama will exterminate the pesky freedom zealots, or the laissez-faire crowds will secede and America's own Europe, North-South Korea, and East-West Germany will develop and gallop to the extents desired. Only thereafter will the Blues have unadulterated occasion to see the sheer moral vacancy of their ways and to consider higher and better ways for people made in God's image. But in no case shall the freeborn stomach another four years of this unmitigated madness or pretend any further by wasting time only to await Hillary taking the reigns in 2017.

Red States already have their own economies, and though strained, they stand in much better shape than do federal balance sheets because of fiscal responsibility and balanced-budget requirements in state constitutions, leaving them without the burdens of runaway debt. With non-federal economies weak but viable, states could quite readily pull their resident-citizens together and go it alone. The enthusiasm and adrenaline over a world thus reopened would infuse seceding states with necessary impetus right from the blocks. The shrugging of smothering federal regulations and tax grabs around every corner would provide for substantially lighter loads upon newly exhilarating journeys. And the monies that feds provide back to the states only represent monies plundered from the states and their residents in the first place. Hence, federal monies will not at all be missed.

Workers will be enlivened, states will drill on their own lands, federal regulations will be lifted, and federal taxation and other schemes will be eliminated. Charity and understanding will be restored, and sound fiscal policy will be instituted to match the expectations of civilized people. The Keystone Pipeline will carry oil flows from Canada through the Red States of North Dakota, South Dakota, Nebraska, Kansas, Oklahoma, and Texas. President Obama and the Blues could then buy oil from the Red States. Though, in a huff, the Blues just might opt for their continuing partnerships with ruthless Saudi Arabia and renegade Venezuela.

Article six of the Constitution provides that, "All Debts... [accrued] before... [the] Constitution shall be valid against the United States under this Constitution, as under the Confederation." This responsible assumption of obligations marks the avenue by which Red States shall also assume their pro-rata share of the runaway debts accumulated by the United States up to the present time. Thereafter, the Reds will set out to pay off and resolve their debts, paying creditors directly and not paying Washington as any sort of go-between. While the Blues will no doubt languish and drown beneath their financial perversions and ignoble schemes, secession will represent nothing short of a gloriously celebrated second Fourth of July in Red States.

The Declaration contemplated "Free and Independent States... Absolved from all Allegiance to the

British Crown…" Furthermore, signatories additionally agreed and advised that "Free and Independent States… have full Power to levy War, conclude Peace, contract Alliances, establish Commerce, and to do all other Acts and Things which Independent States may of right do." Reversion to these principles and arrangements would represent a substantial, independent uptick for each of the Red States, which currently champ at the bit in a rusted, jammed starting gate that now more simulates a holding cell aimed only at robbing and squelching vigorous people who were once prosperous and hopeful.

Obama offers no narrative or plan on spending or on the debt. Democratic leaders have proffered no budget in years. Some want to live in a socialist state. Let them have it. Some want hefty doses of individual liberty for all in order to allow each and every person a shot at their dreams. Let them have it. Secession has become the only alternative to standing around waiting for unreachable agreements and/or even worse compromises. Seeing grand efforts, no progress, and only deep regression in government functioning, honest and reasonable people can see no hope at reconciliation between Red and Blue. It is over.

Why Now?

America tried. She permitted and tolerated much. She weathered plenty. But the time has come to admit to an intractable impasse so deep that it cannot ever be healed. President Obama only pours gasoline on the fire. At this rate, his followers will finish burning the place down on their own via the ballot box even after he leaves office.

The situation will only get worse and worse. A far better course calls for the Reds to secede and for each way of thinking to get its own fair shot to see if it can go its own way and make it work. America no longer has a choice. It must split to save itself at this point. All of the babbling to the contrary is only miserably misguided and unnecessarily and harmfully delaying.

Amazingly, in a country built upon the codified ideals and promises of freedom, great curtailments of freedom have been routinely supported, elected, re-elected, and revered. And even as failure marks the ways of America's God-supplanting government, that government still retains staunch electoral support. And America's voters, now spanning demographic swaths not intended or included by the founders, quite frankly cannot even begin to keep up with the bouncing ball of policy and politics. As a result, these uninformed voters and the political opportunists who prey upon them have ruined the country. Though many have appeared more than happy to live off the fat of the land developed across 240 years of a wisely operated economic nation, failing financial projections spell rapid evaporation of the fat. There simply exists no more time for this welfare state, which remains doggedly entrenched.

President George W. Bush, fighting relatively diminutive enemies abroad, indebted the country by $5 trillion in his eight years. President Obama, giving away money faster than slot machines gone wild, has indebted the country by another $6 trillion in his first four years. Astoundingly, these debt figures represent expenditures beyond the trillions in tax revenues also collected and spent. Ergo, in 12 years the Bush-Obama economic wrecking crew squandered over $11 trillion in borrowed funds, and they more than *tripled* the nation's debt that theretofore had taken 224 years to accumulate! Bush doubled the debt, and Obama did him two better by borrowing even more money in just half the time! These facts and figures stagger and confound any minds paying any attention. Far worse than Osama, Saddam, Muammar, and al-Qaeda, the domestic economic terrorism wrought by back-to-back presidents of opposing parties has indeed brought the United States to the cusp of its own demolition. And now Obama offers more of the same as if his Thelma-and-Louise national death wish cannot be fulfilled quickly enough. Hence, secession cannot come quickly enough either.

Despite a dearth of current mainstream talk of secession, civil war, or electoral alternatives, eagerness for an exit from the Union seethes for many not far beneath the surface. Those who have considered the issues have bided their time to digest 2012's election results, but now all systems are "go," given Obama's victory and the swift resumption of gridlock and irrationality in Washington. Quite simply, a critical mass of the electorate cannot and will not tolerate another four years under President Obama. Too many ingenious, resourceful, self-governing people will simply refuse to honor or tolerate Obama's re-election. The bough must break. And once it does, states will flood from the Union, one after another after another after another. The secession option has ripened. In four more years it will have begun to rot. The time is now.

If time could be frozen, third-party political candidacies and various other experiments might eventually work. For instance, where would the United States stand today had Ross Perot remained steadfast in the 1992 presidential race and beaten Bill Clinton and George H.W. Bush? Perot's Reform Party candidacy of sharp and rational business perspectives would likely be the majority party today. But today, with the clock ticking, the country simply cannot afford to exercise any more patience through the election cycles requisite to develop a smart, successful, and freshly ideated political party. At the 50-state level, time for that has come and gone. Secession remains Americans' only timely option.

States should make decisions from prudence rather than from desperation. In 2013, as bad as things stand, blood and anarchy have not yet come upon the streets. But standing around and waiting for Obama's spending sprees to cripple everyone further would only unnecessarily render secession's course toward a genuine future more chaotic and pressurized. On the other hand, formation of fledgling independent states with a soberly girded citizenry, appropriate laws, and openness for business would provide the best path out of America's current mess. This emergence of independent states could easily be peaceful, agreeable, profitable, and life-, soul-, and freedom-saving.

Surely, with Obama's 2012 victory, all states and all citizens should duck and cover. But many Reds wonder whether to stay the course and hope that a GOP candidate can carry the election in 2016. But even for a Mitt Romney presidency in 2013 or some alternative GOP administration in 2017, without supermajorities in both houses of Congress, the righting of the American ship no longer registers as a legitimate possibility. Even a Republican presidency would be ground down by delay, compromise, decay, a continually muted recovery, and an ultimately failing trajectory. Likely, only a sweeping and publicly supported Gingrich presidency would have had a shot at turning this oversized nation around intact. The reversals and innovations required to salvage America *in toto* remain innumerable. Time, especially against relentlessly drawn-out election cycles and buffeting demographics, has finally slipped away. Even the captain knew, based upon projections from damage already done, that his *Titanic* would sink well before it actually plunged. Similarly, even moderately perceptive people can tell that America will sink based on the widespread wounds (e.g., fiscal, cultural, electoral, political, spiritual) already upon her and the bevy of only muddled options available to her. Wasting any more time, especially when the demographic trend lines spell an undeniable end to America, would be dishonorable and irresponsible for those who know today that time is of the essence and that only one option remains. As the world has survived its prophesied Mayan hurdle in 2012, may Reds turn the page and seek the dawning of a new world in 2013.

According to the Declaration, "Governments… should not be changed for light and transient causes… but when a long train of abuses and usurpations [obtain]… it is right, it is [a] duty, to throw off such Government, and to provide new Guards for… future security…" If only today's leaders were so artfully spoken and determined to confer cherished rights upon others. Remarkably, the Declaration's angst nearly exactly tracks that of Red States in 2013. As America's founders moved swiftly once they decided to break from Great Britain, Reds must also move while they have the chance, especially as the fates of future generations depend upon them.

Overnight, without any further delay, immediately, this afternoon even, Red-State secession could suddenly make everything possible once again. Untouched by bureaucratic nonsense, released from the vise grips of Blue dogma and its rampant stickiness, and emancipated from scanty, godless ideas, Red States could dream again and set upon a course akin to the new-world potentials of 250 years ago. Reds could roll the dice and go for it. They could restore sensibility to governing institutions; they could abrogate and repudiate all impeding notions and vestiges of an America gone wrong. Truly, hearts, minds, and markets would instantaneously reflect the dawning of a new, lively, vibrant, and dream-like age for independent men and women awake enough to set their own courses and vigorous enough to know how to spend God-given gifts and talents in honorable and fruitful ways. This can and must become a reality now. Or all Americans will likely spend the balance of their days treading floodwaters that will envelope and ravage America to no end.

Let the Squawking Begin

The 2012 Obama-Romney options framed only false choices. Those beings on the Earth genetically gifted with 23 chromosomal pairs need not lower themselves by settling for false choices or tolerating bureaucracies or automatons offering them. The Democratic and Republican parties have entirely failed the American people. Added together, they represent a grand total of no choice at all. Both will babble and wrangle with streams of meaningless words over impending secessions, but overwhelming verdicts against these malcontents and corrupt fiduciaries will require citizens to pay them no attention at all.

Yet, predictably, the Blues will loathe and rail against any notion of Red-State secession even though it has not appeared previously that the Blues could abhor anything as much as they have despised the Red States. The Blue reign of terror shall come to an end via secessionist exercises, but the Blues will do what they do best: holler, bluster, whimper, and complain. Red States must discipline themselves to pay the Blues no attention in this regard. The Blues' meal tickets—the Reds—will leave the Blues, and the Blues will have the grand opportunity to taste the bitterness and gall of their own reprehensible policies, their backward worldviews, and their mindless high-five parties heretofore enjoyed upon the backs of others.

Reds must recognize and embrace the overdue words contained herein, further assimilating with every page the unassailable conclusion that Red-State secession stands as the only true choice at this sad and disappointing stage of America's historic tenure. Vehemently, as if they somehow believe their own protestations, Blues will dispute all of this and stomp, kick, and scream in line with the infantile ideology they hold so dear, as long as someone else's mom and dad foot the unwarranted bills. Reds must not fall for it.

With that, here stand six deafening and undeniable signs that secession mercifully beckons on America's otherwise gloomy horizon. These signs sadly highlight America's internal demise. They form the basis on which a pronouncement of death could confidently be made. May all recognize, understand, and heed these signs, and prepare for a true re-emergence of free peoples in newly free societies.

1. A STUPID AND PHONY PRESIDENT

The Declaration, by which Americans broke from Great Britain and its overbearing king, exquisitely expressed the rational and morally superlative stance of free people. Now, amid undeniable and painful ironies, inspired Americans must similarly lodge wholesale charges against President Obama, his ruinous regime, and his indefensible Congressional cronies.

"He has forbidden his Governors to pass Laws of immediate and pressing importance… and… has utterly neglected to attend to them," claimed the colonists in 1776 against a monarch an ocean away. How loudly and uncompromisingly shall American states presently claim the same against the dope in the White House one full reality away?

Pioneering Americans rightly charged the king with "fatiguing them" and leaving their states "exposed to all… dangers, and [to] invasion from without and convulsions within." In 2013, all 50 American states could claim exposure, invasion, and convulsion. For starters, millions upon millions of illegal aliens have invaded America, and the political class remains reluctant to conjure a solution or spring to action lest voting sympathizers recoil at the ballot box. Domestic economies breathe their last gasps, and a fiscal calamity on a scale never before seen beckons with every passing day. This would despondently parallel Rome's historic meltdown, if only America's president mustered his turn at the fiddle. Rather, as was also legibly and forcefully charged in 1776, Obama has "erected a multitude of New Offices… [and] swarms of Officers to harass our people, [to] eat out our substance..., [and to] impose taxes on us without our consent." These words formerly roused free people to action. Today, a largely subdued people nod their heads in agreement with these indictments one moment only to return to their semi-lobotomized stations in life in the next moment.

As if this emasculation were not enough, the king, the president, and their ilk have likewise set about "abolishing our most valuable Laws, and altering fundamentally the Forms of our Governments" (Declaration of Independence). Placement of *politically* inclined minds upon the high court, erosion of the Constitution via ravenous Supreme Court inventions (e.g., in *Roe v. Wade* in 1973 and in the Affordable Care Act ruling in 2012), and incessant and unexplained borrowing and spending at careless and catastrophic levels constitute modern-day excesses of maniacal leadership untethered from reason or responsibility.

With too few literary adjectives in existence, proper and fitting excoriation of the Obama presidency cannot adequately be expressed upon any number of printed pages. Off the top, the following come to the fore: vacuous, incoherent, oblivious, counterfeit, insecure, embarrassing, thin, godless, inbred, childish, redundant, boring, impotent, unteachable, self-deluded, deceitful, artless, exhausted, and small. True and right, even these wide-ranging descriptions fail miserably to capture or verbalize the contemptibility of the Obama presidency. Only an unprintable and inexpressible visceral upheaval measured in grunts, groans, and entrails could ever adequately describe the disaster at the White House.

No doubt, well before 2008 ears grew quite weary of President George W. Bush's redundancy and intransigence. Across eight largely inarticulate years, most with sense eventually stopped believing that fresh solutions could anymore emanate from the Bush White House. Unfortunately, soon after Obama's national honeymoon ended in 2009, it also became astoundingly clear that this new president had nothing to say, nothing to offer, and would only set out to gut and debone hard-won national fruits and treasures (e.g., space, charity, goodwill, progress, defense, respect, prosperity, opportunity).

The Obama years have showcased the most absurd administration not only in history but in imagination. The excessively careless promises made after seizing power (e.g., transparency of lawmaking and deficit halving) receive absolutely zero acknowledgment by the president today, let alone earnest explanation or cogent reconciliation. This executive branch has strayed so far from the bounds and standards of decency and competence that any and all level-headed people have long ago given up looking for any promising signs of hope. Basically, America has been set adrift in the open sea. Worse yet, nobody acknowledges this or seeks to rectify it, no matter how bad the seasickness gets or how great the make-up distance grows between America and the nearest port. Still worse, this carnival has just been re-elected.

This book hardly provides support to the candidacy of Mitt Romney or to the Republican Party. In fact, Republican neglect and incompetence birthed the Obama presidency. At issue, however, is the fact that had a plain paper plate run for president in 2012, it should have beaten President Obama by at least 100 percentage points. Any nameless, faceless, colorless, generic candidate who would dare to place the Obama years on trial should have won every single vote and then some. That this did not happen only forewarns of impending doom.

Is President Obama smart? His unrehearsed syllables (e.g., "um," and "uh," and "hmmm," and "let me be clear") drip with a stunning lack of intellect. The president's freakish reliance on teleprompters not only continues unabated but still receives no explanation despite it becoming the ongoing butt of wisecracks and concerns for years. The concealment of academic records, the avoidance of legitimate media, and the incessant deceiving, distorting, and lying (e.g., the cover-up of the president's inaction during the siege against the U.S. embassy in Benghazi, Libya, and the countless 2012 campaign falsehoods lodged against Romney) only serve to fortify the conclusion that a numbskull has somehow made it to the Oval Office for an eight-year stay smack-dab in the middle of America's dimmest hours.

The Ice-Cream Man

The stupid aspects of the Obama presidency are best felt by the American people languishing behind and beneath his cluelessness. Americans have been reduced to living in the slow lane, piled up behind a meandering ice-cream truck making its leisurely neighborhood rounds, where the ice-cream man himself remains infamously unaware of his bulkiness and his inability to get out of his own or anybody else's way. The country's self-imposed inanity requires playing nice and pretending that Obama is a real president, no matter how obviously his emptiness obstructs and how unbelievably his vacancy leaves him unable to hear the horns rightly honking behind him. What kind of people tolerates such absurdities? The country, built up and rightfully vaunted over the course of two centuries, has been devastated by a grand backwardness taking power at a most critical point in history. And yet, quite weirdly, the people endure it.

President Obama "leads" this once-radiant country as if it were a Third World start-up. Loosey goosey, Obama drones on and on regarding trivial matters (e.g., the Bush tax cuts, the supposed fiscal cliff, the supposed sequester), and then, having persuaded a grand total of zero people, he compromises by agreeing to some casual, random, and temporary fix that is really no fix at all. By doing this over and over and over and over, the president unwittingly announces to the entire world that he not only has zero idea in which country he resides, but that he also has zero clue as to how most rational human beings make even semi-sophisticated decisions across time horizons extending beyond the next meal, statutory expiration, or election cycle. Just the cartoonish nature of such governance skewers any and all hope that the president could ever learn or gain any idea as to how the real world of thoughtful and considerate planning operates. The blankness of the administration on these issues has predictably resulted in shrewd people delaying meaningful decisions until a real administration takes power, the possibility of which has alarmingly drifted out of sight. Though the president once famously cautioned against gambling in Las Vegas, any old and crusty roulette wheel would easily provide better odds and predictabilities than does the Obama regime in responsibly mapping plans for authentic human living. But there is no escaping this quagmire because the ice-cream man cannot ever learn enough just to get out of the way.

Doling out goodies certainly does seem to excite bloc votes from simpletons, thereby conferring public powers to popular clowns. And this racket will surely feather Obama's nest for life, even as the country sinks and even as his frenzied supporters are no better off, not that they would ever notice. This poisonous dynamic presents a crude shell game where the honorable and honest pay dearly for everything and yet the nation still plummets. Find enough fools and the game is rigged in favor of the candidate with the fewest moral qualms and the most quarts of Haagen-Dazs. Proven in 2008 and 2012, the United States finally and verifiably contains enough fools to empower someone as downright vacant as Obama.

And so America sits there behind the ice-cream man in his oversized, single- geared, puttering sugar truck. He offers sweets to the addicted and waves to the undiscerning. The rest of the people have been playing along as nicely as possible, pretending as best they could that the ice-cream man had the wherewithal to be, well, a president. Tolerating and weathering the nightmare as nice people do, nobody wanted to offend. Until now.

Manchurian President

The phony nature of the Obama administration stems from the great scarcity of evidence that President Obama actually understands the issues and makes the decisions attributed to him. In fact, anybody impartially watching the shenanigans in Washington must admit to the eerie parallel between Obama's illegitimacy and that of literature's *Manchurian Candidate.* For both Manchurians simply do as others have directed them behind the scenes. Without explanation, remorse, or any sense of awareness, Manchurian Obama just proceeds to golf, vacation, campaign, fundraise, and read words fed to him by others while the country swirls the drain. No matter how embarrassing or humiliating these rote and simple activities become, Obama just motors along as if these are not disgraceful accumulations. Weirdly, Obama has not released his college or law-school grades or work product. Prior presidents have routinely released such information because they respected the office and the people. Though grades have not always been stellar for Oval-Office occupants, the people have always been gracious and understanding, realizing that there is always more to a person than school grades from years ago. But mysteriously in Obama's case, there is always less and less. Obama has managed to prove himself nothing but a Manchurian by his listlessness, his aloofness, his strangely revealing off-script utterances, and his resounding lack of conscience or awakening. Even his cat-and-mouse games with his birth certificate only served to demonstrate humiliating juvenility and an ever-alarming smallness within the *most powerful man on Earth.*

That he would, without fail, continue for six straight years (two campaigning and four as president) to read grammatical errors as written, distortions as scripted, lies as directed, and redundancies as catered, only proves the fit of the Manchurian label. Again, the only thing worse than these shocking maladies continues to be the president's total lack of self-recognition, his lack of any hint of a learning curve, and the expired hope of his snapping out of any of this.

Further, Manchurian Obama has gone so far as to prove himself to be America's first affirmative-action president (i.e., preferred but unqualified) and her first hunter-gatherer president (i.e., propagating uncertain, piecemeal existences). While neither moniker has historically qualified anybody for any kind of leadership, let alone for the presidency of the United States, standards in 2008 and 2012 so plummeted that dignity and decency themselves jumped from the cliffs, leaving the Oval Office entirely up for grabs.

Nothing of what Obama says, writes, reads aloud, or does provides any remarkable indication of noteworthy aptitude or any independent or critical thought. Indefensible and embarrassing, Obama and the Blues pay this alarming fact no attention at all. Zip. Nil. Nada. If any of these foregoing assessments miss the mark, it remains incumbent upon the president to establish such by exhibiting anything smacking of personal aptitude and not reminiscent of handler interventions and excuses.

Throughout the entirety of the Obama administration's tenure, trillions of privately held dollars have been sitting idly by while their owners have been endlessly scratching their heads trying to figure out what surprise the White House will next break out of its paralyzing bag of tricks. This hunter-gatherer president exhibits not a clue as to how modern and sophisticated societies plan, investigate, decide, and operate. Rather, the president operates within a moment-to-moment, procrastinating, uncertain, unreliable, guessing game upon an overly reduced playing field wherein transformative ideas have been banished. This scheme may have worked just fine for cavemen, but for idealistic and realistic Americans this marks a comprehensive undoing of advanced civilization and a regrettable retracement of thousands of years of history.

Following the lead of the nation's first Manchurian president has simply become too much to bear, especially in light of the irresponsible yet multiplying electorate that appointed him and still mindlessly applauds him.

What can be concluded? The president himself forces observers to reach stark verdicts because he never outlines or shares his thought processes or rational bases for his supposed conclusions and decisions. Thus, either he has absolutely no clue and is the Manchurian President, or he simply disrespects himself, his Maker, and the people to no end by hiding in the shadows, too unwilling to explain himself. With plenty of evidence in the books, the former characterization seems at this point the more plausible—that Obama is simply the Manchurian fruition long feared.

Six Words

Having a stupid president is bad. Having a phony president is worse. But perhaps the greatest pain facing Reds lies in their deep and daily visceral angst over the hijacking of their country and the elimination of what would have been their children's country. That grievous pain can perhaps best be conveyed through an example of how even six seemingly innocuous words do so easily torture those who loved old America.

Day by day in America 2012, news accounts took hourly stock of the presidential campaign between Obama and Romney. On its face, this coverage featured a narrative that very wrongly legitimized the Obama presidency. For example, news reporters would say and citizens would hear things like, "President Obama campaigned in Ohio today…" For the engaged and reflective, these six words alone prove simply indigestible. Before even uttering the words "President Obama," any self-respecting newsman should warn viewers, as customarily done when showing carnage, that the following report may turn stomachs, dampen spirits, and insult intelligence. Rattling off words following the gasp-worthy prefix "President Obama" at best smacks of journalistic naïveté but more likely represents the thoughtless work of an oblivious, desensitized marionette just happy to be on the air or in print.

Continuing with the six words: after suffering through yet another wrongly casual mention of the contented ruiner of this once-great country (with the aiding and abetting of millions of fellow ruiners), the word "campaigned" flows with a thud for anyone really attuned. "Campaigned"? Seriously? How in the world has someone with President Obama's record not been hospitalized for uncontrollable blushing? Should not the top story concern the super-human strength the president has demonstrated in even being able to stand upright given his appalling turn in the White House? This piecemeal, fly-by-night, visionless operation cannot be defended by anyone with standards. How have "reporters" failed to ask why the president seems so unaffected even after wreaking havoc upon what used to be the most powerful and prestigious of nations?

What kind of on-air automaton could skip right past the word "campaigned" without pausing to acknowledge the insanity of it all? In an appropriate world, news stories would not only query why President Obama has failed to apologize profusely to America and to the world, but why in the realm of plausibility did President Obama not step down when he first realized that the nation needed a leader and that he was not it. An ancillary story should examine how anyone could support such a tragic president whose train wreck of an administration has relentlessly, soullessly, precipitously, and ruthlessly devastated the very recognizability of the country contemplated in its long-forsaken, original founding documents.

While books could be written on the six words alone, the last three, "in Ohio today," highlight how America has devolved into a ham-handed, mish-mashed operation that only seasonally kowtows to battleground states to get the keys to the machines to torture the rest of the states year-round. How can the president be in Ohio and not first be called to account for the Blues' economic deforestation of the "heart of it all"? "Today" establishes that the president would presumably be on the move to spread lies, false concerns, and general joylessness to other places tomorrow and the next day. America has degenerated into a place where few pay attention to what anyone says, and almost no one considers even his own words. In a day long ago, actual journalists and active voters would have demanded something other than routinely shallow coverage of a president's superficial, cotton-candy blow through town.

2. A SPASTICALLY UNRELIABLE ELECTORATE

America needs a cure. On the brink, she cannot at all survive on her present course. And yet her voters refuse to hear her, help her, or heal her. Spastically unreliable, the electorate largely pays America no attention at all. Rather, it votes instinctively for its self-centered, short-term, and ever-weirder interests regardless of the dire consequences.

Since Bill Clinton's easy re-election in 1996, and starting with the 2000 cliffhanger where George W. Bush defeated reigning Vice President Al Gore, the American electorate has been locked in a near-50-50 hardening of positions. Consequently, American elections and politics now routinely bear likeness to the Cuban Missile Crisis, where any blinking or yielding before the enemy simply cannot be survived. In actuality, through the fine-tuning of campaigns, the statistical research concerning one-issue voters, longstanding party-loyalty reliance, and the coddling of the vagaries of independent voters, political parties have internally compromised to make their electoral triumphs possible but not to make governing plausible. Zeroed in to the very last of the bean counting, candidates and their puppet-master "handlers" can no longer exit the campaign superhighway and turn their attentions to governance. With political processes so thinned and gutted of issue leadership, the system has been rendered useless in any practical, ruling sense. For example, presidential candidates and campaigns visit only undecided battleground states, where issues have been narrowed, trimmed, and reduced so as to make even Michael Jackson's infamously disappearing nose full-figured in comparison. No common-sense candidate has a place in politics anymore. For who with a straight face could go on pretending that this in any way pays homage or heed to the brilliant and noble visions surrounding the nation's inception?

The country ebbs beneath grave troubles that cannot even begin to be overstated, let alone calculated. And relative to her potential and promise, America has been annihilated by wanton dunderheads running for office and by their empty-headed and selfish-hearted accomplices at the ballot box.

Nowhere in the Constitution, in the Declaration, or in the Bible are free people required to pretend that self-destructively false choices are somehow otherwise. But even in the clear case of the lesser of two evils (i.e., Republicans and Democrats), America obviously cannot get it right anymore. For example, though a substantially superior prospective leader than President Obama, inoffensive 2012 Republican challenger Mitt Romney could not even get elected. Surely, not even Ronald Reagan or Abraham Lincoln would get their opportunities to man the tiller and navigate the country to safe, emancipated, and prosperous waters these days because neither could ever get elected in today's America where half of the citizenry cares so little about liberation to begin with. Freedom registers first and foremost only in the hearts and minds of those diminishing numbers of zealots long ago contemplated in the founding documents. Today, a freedom agenda can no longer be politically enacted. Sadly, it stirs too little interest or enthusiasm. Only compromised schemes destined to slow-bleed the country to death ever gather enough support for national legislative enactments or for electoral victories.

New Demographic Realities

Margaret Thatcher, Great Britain's prime minister from 1979 to 1991, openly and rightly marveled at the Anglo-Saxons who historically refused to live separated from self-determination. She saw them as set apart from other peoples of the world in this regard. And so, if Thatcher is correct, perhaps individual freedoms are quite simply not that big of a deal to most people, including various peoples of America. Accordingly, Republicans have historically relied upon low voter turnout in order to win presidential elections. And with remarkable regularity, Republicans succeeded, as those disinterested in politics remained distant from election-day polling locales. But now, President Obama has awakened the masses, advised them where and how to take hold of the cookie jar, and called on them to vote for perpetual replenishment of the jar at the expense of everyone else. While policy arguments and the issues of a nation may have long failed to stir the masses historically, the cookie jar surely arouses them today. Now, holding the jar, controlling its access codes, and emptying and refilling the jar at world-record paces, Obama and his masses have in short order signaled the end of America. Spastic in their proclivities, cookie lovers have become dogmatically Blue regardless of the facts, the stakes, or the costs. This raw spasticity has been illuminated through exit polls and voter interviews. Questioning the grounds for Blue voting decisions generally elicits only horrifying discoveries that no sound reasoning even exists in the minds of most of these lever pullers.

Factually and irrespective of efficacy, the populist demise of the Reds and the rising tide of the Blues have long been foreshadowed across a series of constitutional amendments, which marked distinct and defying departures from America's founding documents and rationales. The 15th Amendment in 1870 extended the vote to all races of men. Of course, non-White men overwhelmingly vote Blue. The 16th Amendment in 1913 established the income tax whereby moneymaking taxpayers would be coerced to underwrite almost everything. Not surprisingly, in short order an albatross of a government emerged and, bent upon appeasing and winning favor of shallowly partisan votes, utilized the lure and promise of monetary kickbacks now constitutionally seized from others. These monetary recipients almost exclusively vote Blue. The 19th Amendment in 1920 granted the vote to women. The "gender gap" has since demarcated the margins by which women disproportionately vote Blue. The 24th Amendment in 1964 eliminated poll taxes across various states. This eliminated any costs associated with voting, which had previously tempered Blue votes. The 26th Amendment in 1971 reduced the voting age from 21 years to 18 years.

Of course, these younger voters, often green and wide-eyed, most susceptibly vote for the simplest of solutions, which invariably emanate from the Blues. As if all of these developments were not enough, in 2012 President Obama lip-served a variety of well-calculated, impromptu positions in order to entice single-issue voters to his side. This ultimately worked to deliver his narrow re-election "victory."

The halcyon days of Ronald Reagan have rapidly and widely escaped America. The electorate can no longer be swayed by cogent or compelling argument or by genuine statesmanship. Rather it has become largely unresponsive to stimuli. New developments, emergent facts, and dire needs now routinely fail to inspire or goad Blue voters particularly. No matter how unobjectionable and accommodating the Red candidate for president, this electorate will vote Blue. Myopic, today's electing majority ensures that the Reds shall never run the country again.

Worse than the deplorable but temporary Obama presidency, the electorate that brought this administration to power in 2008 and then inconceivably renewed its demolition permit in 2012 has undergone multi-generational and irreversible shifts, which have now effectively terminated the age of meaningful elections in America. While Obama should have run 100 points behind even a masked unknown, this electorate born of new demographics not only shockingly chose Obama but also promises, given the chance, to plunge the country into the cesspool of other base, gravity-laden, animalistic societies even after Obama exits the White House. Accordingly, Obama is more properly viewed as an alarming *symptom* of a greater and permanent electoral *problem.*

The facts are these: only a majority of White voters support Reds; all other ethnicities overwhelmingly vote for Blues. With 93-96% of Black voters, 73% of Asian voters, and 71% of Hispanic voters supporting Obama, America has reached the point where only Blues can win the White House. Such glum prospects mark the effective demise of the essential conservative principles and policies that underwrote and undergirded the unprecedented success of America's two-and-a-half-century monopoly on its high-grade brand of freedom, innovation, affluence, and leadership. Unappreciated and misunderstood, America's conservative history now miserably fails to energize the gimme-gimme, me-first yelps of today's coldly debilitating voters. Content to dillydally with the nation's trinkets and to proceed unduly consumptive of the nation's goodwill and accumulated riches, these latest generations appear unwilling to carry the torch that has now passed to them. The incomprehensibly spastic and inflexible electoral support for President Obama provides unmistakable writing on the wall that America, as presently constituted, will go up in smoke, while superior ideas, honorable actions, reliable systems, and the people who offer and shoulder them will forever be outvoted to death.

In 21st-century America, only one in four Black children is born to married parents. Of Hispanic children, fewer than one in two are born to married parents. How much have these cancerous statistics been discussed, debated, and overcome in public discourse and with this current president? Not at all! The Blue machinery counts the Black vote in its corner; the Black vote delivers election after election; and Black America declines and crumbles further as if such were its destiny. And now more and more, Hispanic voters are similarly expected to deliver Blue candidates the votes they need. These Hispanic voters will also get nothing meaningful or durable from the Blues in return. Partly as a result of these dire familial statistics, Black and Hispanic children gravely underperform their White and Asian peers in school, and the vicious cycle continues unabated. No matter, Blacks and Hispanics continue to vote Blue at any cost and will seemingly do so until the end of time.

Hispanic Americans constitute the nation's fastest-growing demographic group with population projections far outpacing every other ethnicity. And with upwards of 12 million illegal aliens in the country (most presumably of Hispanic descent), the nation's "leaders" have historically gone mum—willfully crippled in what to do about the problem for fear that the Hispanic voting populations will backlash against those not treating *illegal* immigrants sweetly and gently. Anemic, emasculated, and surrendered, the country has essentially yielded to an invasion by illegal immigrants and their presumed camaraderie with voting citizens. And while the state of Arizona dared to police its own border and territory against this odd political teamwork, the federal government successfully sued to keep the Grand Canyon State occupied, hogtied, excoriated, and helpless. Arizona will be on a morphine drip of an existence in due time as its Red history, ideals, and electoral margins erode day by day.

In addition to Black and Hispanic votes against Reds, the gender gap (whereby women vote Blue and men vote Red) has only intensified, as the electorate has now become 54% female. Beyond that, Blues continue more and more to target single-issue voters however and wherever necessary, with gay marriage and free contraceptive access being Obama's latest ploy in 2012.

Frenetic trends and ever-creeping hullaballoo favor Blues and make it look as if the Red States will never again cast their electoral votes for anyone who actually becomes president. And there is no stopping this runaway electoral train. Not even the facts can slow the madness.

The country of France now toys with a 75% income-tax rate on the wealthy to pay for its Blue existence. President Jimmy Carter featured 70% marginal tax rates in his day and carelessly crippled America with his Blue agenda. President Reagan then cut those rates to 28% and restored America to its robust potential. But unfortunately, of today's lot, not enough people remember, understand, or care how it has largely taken Red policies to reverse Blue disasters. Alarmingly, neither outlandish French considerations nor Carter's ruinous policies even register with Blue Americans. For Blues seemingly cannot be bothered with such information or consideration. Spastic and catatonic, they appear to have no interest in understanding.

Constitutional amendments long after the nation's principled founding have given the vote to citizens regardless of moral turpitude, brainpower, participation, or any other factor relating to electoral competence. Interestingly, driving a car, tending bar, and welding metals require passage of examinations, certification, and proficiency. Yet, how backward have America's standards become that voting requires no such effort or grasp at all? In a country founded upon the invitation of moral citizens to join a society of unchained individuals, subsequent amendments and the commensurate influx of unlike-minded citizens have transformed America into parallels of other average nations and far from the burgeoning frontier once envisioned, witnessed, revered, and protected.

Demographic trends and their voting propensities doom continuation of America's formerly prosperous processes. Unassailable, yet no doubt destined to provoke unintelligible rage, these assessments will continue to prove true day after day after day.

Following the 2012 election, the Republican mainstream began murmuring of tempering its message, luring Hispanic voters, adjusting to a new norm (a soft electorate voting increasingly Blue in presidential elections), nitpicking the Romney candidacy, overcoming the press, retooling the primary season, and on and on. Of course, a grand total of none of these strategies matters or will ever really matter. The demographic course has been set, and its voting patterns will not change. Look around the world. Where, oh where do Red perspectives win elections? Nowhere. In addition to that unconquerable obstacle, Reds must realize that captors of cookie jars hardly ever give them back due to any subsequent enlightenment. Robbers and self-seekers usually stay dim for quite a while—as in forever—save for an authentic spiritual conversion.

Insane Results

America's crumbling electorate has erected a political class with horrifying results. The Constitution (Article 4, Section 4) provides that "The United States shall guarantee to every State in this Union a Republican Form of Government, and shall protect each of them against Invasion; and on Application of the Legislature, or of the Executive (when the Legislature cannot be convened) against domestic Violence." How neglectfully, forgetfully, and/or criminally has the federal government today forsaken these protections? Not only have the feds not protected the states from invasion (e.g., rampant and debilitating illegal immigration), they have also sued states determined to protect themselves from invasion. Applying salt to these wounds, the detached and loopy courts have incomprehensibly upheld such roping of the states. And everyone seems just fine with it all.

In addition, the federally heavy-handed usurpation of monies followed by the gradual, trick-requiring feedback of those monies to the states, local governments, and communities far more mimics a road-show circus of tricks and treats than any nation the founding documents ever foretold. The feds not only fail to protect the states as constitutionally required, they also raid citizen and business coffers across the states in order to play Robin Hood in favor of those willing to vote Blue and go with the lollygagging flow.

Further, the 5th Amendment (from 1791) to the Constitution provides that, "No person… be deprived of life, liberty, or property, without due process of law." Of course, this essential protection was wholly hijacked by the subsequently misguided 16th Amendment (from 1913) providing for an income tax. Thereafter, willy-nilly, the feds have been empowered to tinker with, threaten over, and argue about what atrocities they will next bring to bear with the most insane tax code known to any civilization anywhere, ever. With simple-majority votes, the feds can and do plunder productive citizens via the tax code, though prohibition of such exploitation was presumably ensured originally in order to lure the states to the Union.

While the elected Blues take and plot, gather and scheme, the elected "Reds" sleep and yield, slumber and apologize. Meanwhile, the country founded upon the greatest of individual liberties regresses beneath the monotony of Lilliputian minds (i.e., Republicans and Democrats) fake fighting in tiny arenas (e.g., disingenuous Congressional floors) over beggarly purses (e.g., 2012's puny "fiscal cliff") before stunted crowds of no discernment (i.e., spastic and unreliable voters). Surely, America used to be bigger than that!

The United States represents an utterly sinking ship. With over $16 trillion in debt, Obama's runaway spending, and Congress's impotence and spinal void, the country has ground to a halt, solely awaiting cessation of breathing. Meanwhile, even the people paying some sort of attention naively put their hope in the next election and the prospect of new "leadership." This goes to show how gullible the populace has become. Imagine even a Romney victory and a Republican Senate and House. Can anyone actually conceive of even that government reversing the current course to the extent necessary? Would not the yelping and moaning of the selfish prevail once again in scaring the always-cowardly GOP? Would not the next campaign cycle quickly cut short any meaningful progress? Would not Blue filibusters in the Senate preserve the poison pills the nation has already consumed? The post-hoc wrangling and debating over the 2012 election just showed how out-of-touch with reality even the observant have become.

Greatly exacerbating the backward system of US federal governance, bizarre incentives reward the irresponsible while penalizing the responsible. For example, reports now show that college graduates have been delaying marriage in order to prioritize the pay-down of their student loans. Of course, this results in college graduates having fewer children as they experience later starts in matrimony compared to generations past. While fewer are the offspring of the college-educated, more numerous are the offspring of the high-school dropouts where government's financial-assistance programs based upon family size continue unabated. American impotence in dealing with these nauseatingly upside-down policies has finally come home to roost in two excruciating locales: at the ballot box where the unlearned, untaxed, and publicly funded vote in near lockstep for propagation of policies cursed from Heaven and doomed on Earth, and in the budget where not even national defense can be afforded, given the outlay to care for those who refuse to care for themselves.

The 2012 presidential election highlighted the height of American insanity. President Obama has been by far the worst president imaginable. He has made no sense and has given zero impression that any of "his" words are his own, that "his" thoughts are his own, or that "his" decisions are his own. On the other hand, there has likely never been a candidate as squeaky clean as Romney. A family man, splendid student, successful businessman, and philanthropist, Romney appeared clearly beyond reproach. Older and wiser, Romney's unflappable strength, humanity, and resolve should have engendered and not hindered. Beyond all of that, Romney clearly had zero personal need for the presidency. He appears to have sufficient family, resource, and peace to do whatever he wishes for the rest of his days. Nowhere does any inkling arise indicating power hunger or ulterior motives in Romney's seeking of the White House.

And so, if the cleanest candidate in history could not resoundingly trounce at the polls the worst, most destructive, and bafflingly nonsensical president in history, then America has completely come apart and must be rebuilt for real! Surely, since the Reagan years, America has taken a catastrophic leave of her senses. As a result, nobody to the right of Bill Clinton will ever be elected president again. Thus, short of undergoing a majority-pleasing political emasculation, Reds will never win the presidency across the currently aligned 50 states.

The tide has turned and will only turn faster still. Demographic projections show this catastrophe to be headed rather steeply downhill. Even worse, the ignorance and spastic nature of the voters portends against reversal of Blue political leanings.

This spastic nature was again proven when challenger Romney led Obama slightly in "likely voter" polls in September of 2012 and former President Bill Clinton strode to the podium at the Democratic National Convention and declared that nobody, not even he, could have fixed in four short years the mess inherited by Obama. This bogus assessment by a once-moderate president became the instant and rejuvenating mantra of the languishing Obama campaign. It provided an excuse for presidential failure. The next night, Obama gave an emboldened retread of a speech, which appeared to energize knee-jerk voters incapable of sensing the inappropriateness of a sitting president expounding upon the sad state of national affairs in his push for re-election as if he had not had the chance to fix these things already. As an aside in response to Clinton's election-altering point, of course Reagan inherited a much worse economy in 1981 than Obama inherited in 2009, and yet Reagan entirely turned things around by the middle of his first term. It took vision, sense, leadership, and competence. Nonetheless, Clinton's words reigned. Reagan was forgotten. Romney and company went mute. And all of a sudden, Obama surged to leads even in "likely voter" polls. So went the campaign in 2012, most recently demonstrating how presidential politics have slipped beyond the bounds and reach of reason, and how elections can no longer deliver America.

3. WRONGNESS: THE HOMOSEXUAL EXAMPLE

President Obama came out in favor of gay marriage and a host of gay rights during his 2012 re-election campaign. He did this to siphon White support from one-issue voters on the subject and because he has no understanding of the topic of homosexuality. In the aftermath of the president's maneuvering, the gay-rights movement has taken wing to the point that much of the country murmurs Joan Cusack's Emily Montgomery line from 1997's *In and Out*: "Is everybody gay?" The largely unopposed homosexual onslaught marks an immoral society coming apart. But just as disturbing, and the focus of this chapter, the blanket acceptance of homosexuality marks a society without any relevant understanding. Continuing ignorance in this regard will require a staunch refusal to learn the truths unveiled in the pages ahead. While the fates of Sodom and Gomorrah await the immoral naysayers, the willfully ignorant will suffer a wholly avoidable gauntlet of their own. Perhaps illuminating the wrongness of the pro-homosexual movement will open minds to seek understanding first and to adopt positions of advocacy only thereafter.

Many Blue assumptions run so counter to reality that resultant Blue policies meet with the same ineffectiveness that would have resulted had such efforts been sprawled randomly across the abyss of space. Such misguided endeavors routinely cost trillions of dollars, help nobody, diminish everybody, and yet seek rubber-stamped renewal and replenishment as if the disturbing results have somehow been concealed. This tragic and redundant course has already poisoned K-12 education, bankrupted America but for her greenback printing presses and self-mortgage to China, lulled masses into a permanent underclass and voting bloc, and wasted vast human resources upon senseless arguments moment after moment and year by year. This chapter takes sharp aim at but one of these Blue misfires. Wrong on its premises, rash in its solutions, cold in its implementation, and vacant in its conscience, Blue ideology fails across the board in nearly everything it touches. This solitary example of homosexuality, emblematic of many others, shall serve to illustrate the depth of stunning and rampant Blue cluelessness.

This chapter stems not from offense, activism, or agenda. It aims high, shoots straight, and lets the chips fall. The bona fides of its author stand readily available. With loyalty toward all rather than favoritism for any, this chapter isolates and identifies the activating mechanisms of homosexuality and considers the fallout in light of the superficial Blue treatment of the topic.

In this discussion, non-issues are vanquished, Scriptural truths elucidated, and implications mentioned. Piercing the confused din of public opinion, this chapter supplies missing puzzle pieces for those seeking truth and understanding.

Non-Issues

From nature-nurture conundrums to congenital-versus-choice debates, and from genetic code inquiries to Lady Gaga's "Born This Way," controversy coalesces around homosexuality's underlying causations and corollary blames. This analysis, for the sake of argument among other reasons, readily concedes existence of disparate and innate propensities toward homosexuality. Readers may readily assume as correct the natural, congenital, genetic, Lady Gaga positions on homosexuality's etiology. Likewise, dissenters may assume alternatively that homosexuality arises in and from nurture, choice, and experience, including socialization mores and norms, molestation, sexual abuse, modeling of abusive behavior, and any longing for belonging, or any other latest, greatest explanation.

Rigidly, debate has largely centered within the innate/choice dichotomy where conclusions as to causation generally direct subsequent positions and policy recommendations. For example, those convinced of homosexuality's natural emergence would more likely tend to be tolerant of those engaging in behavior consistent with such physiological constitutions. Conversely, those who consider homosexuality to arise from choice may trend more strictly in judgment and disapproval, given the lack of biological imperatives or urges.

Now, having given time and attention to the

foregoing, none of it matters at all. Neither position is right or relevant. Assumption of either position shall be rendered a nullity. The actual triggering and activating mechanisms of homosexuality and its commensurate behaviors emerge avoidably elsewhere.

Scriptures

Another thesis for another time will take to task those who have cosmetically quoted Scripture to dispense cheaply of the homosexuality debate with casual concern for the ripple effects of such superficial resolutions. Worse than atheists, willfully shallow users of the Bible muffle and cloud questions and answers. Solely citing Leviticus in 2013 with its zero-tolerance laws only illustrates a lack of understanding or appreciation of other, more illuminative verses in the era of Christ.

That said, clues regarding homosexuality's activation lie nestled within Romans 1:18-32:

> **18** The wrath of God is being revealed
> from Heaven against all the godlessness
> and wickedness of men, who suppress the
> truth by their wickedness, **19** since what
> may be known about God is plain to
> them, because God has made it plain to
> them. **20** For since the creation of the
> world God's invisible qualities—His
> eternal power and divine nature—have
> been clearly seen, being understood from
> what has been made, so that men are
> without excuse.

21 For although they knew God, they
neither glorified Him as God nor gave
thanks to Him, but their thinking became
futile and their foolish hearts were
darkened. **22** Although they claimed to be
wise, they became fools **23** and exchanged
the glory of the immortal God for images
made to look like a mortal man and birds
and animals and reptiles.
24 Therefore God gave them over in the
sinful desires of their hearts to sexual
impurity for the degrading of their bodies
with one another. **25** They exchanged the
truth about God for a lie, and worshiped
and served created things rather than the
Creator—who is forever praised. Amen.
26 Because of this, God gave them over
to shameful lusts. Even their women
exchanged natural relations for unnatural
ones. **27** In the same way the men also
abandoned natural relations with women
and were inflamed with lust for one
another. Men committed indecent acts
with other men, and received in
themselves the due penalty for their
perversion.
28 Furthermore, since they did not think
it worthwhile to retain the knowledge of
God, He gave them over to a depraved
mind, to do what ought not to be done.
29 They have become filled with every
kind of wickedness, evil, greed and
depravity. They are full of envy, murder,
strife, deceit and malice. They are gossips,

> **30** slanderers, God-haters, insolent, arrogant and boastful; they invent ways of doing evil; they disobey their parents;
> **31** they are senseless, faithless, heartless, ruthless. **32** Although they know God's righteous decree that those who do such things deserve death, they not only continue to do these very things but also approve of those who practice them.

While verses 26-27 condemn homosexuality, preceding and subsequent verses place the matter beneath well-lit microscopes such that each and every person, not just those with homosexual leanings, may understand and relate.

Verse 18 unveils a present-tense wrath against all godlessness and wickedness (e.g., deceit, cowardice, selfishness, pride, etc.). For kickers, suppression of the truth, man's all-time favorite, goes unappreciated from Heaven in that same initial verse. Beware.

Next, verses 19-20 demonstrate that awareness and knowledge of God flows not from mere dispensations of fellow men. Rather, God has opted to make Himself plain to each person through, at a minimum, daily revelation available from simple observations of what God has made. God insists that those viewing or examining the sun, the moon, the stars, the peaks of the Himalayas, seasons, symmetries, or even something as simple as water acknowledge inherent magnificence and humble themselves in ways befitting awe and proper perspective. At the end of verse 20, the Scriptures contemplate each person being without excuse for missing this.

Of course, man has become expert at paying little to

no attention whenever he so desires. As a result, subsequent verses show an uptick in the stakes along with a noticeable simmer. Despite being fitted with the remarkable wherewithal to know God personally, man stubbornly persists in not glorifying God as God and in not being grateful (verse 21). Rather, man commences prideful thinking on subjects only breeding greater futility, like the homosexuality debate itself or efforts to cure poverty, and as a result hearts become needlessly frustrated and darkened. How much punishment does ingratitude warrant? What of deliberate refusal and forsaking of a knowable, engaging God? What price must be paid for expending human thought upon unworkable puzzles and accepting the hardening and dimming of the human heart?

Continuing along, God patiently allows man to work it out and learn the hard way, if necessary. So, what does man do with this opportunity? As verses 22-23 reveal, man claims his own wisdom, becomes a fool (the evidence of which lies obviously in the darkness of common, secretive, underground lives), and trades God for more manageable images and conceptions. What an absolute spiritual cataclysm this represents.

As the next series of verses explains, man, ripe for correction and rebuke, receives from God a series of alarms aimed to awaken and restore. Some lives meander, immersed in commonly sinful shenanigans like drunkenness. Other lives fall prey to repulsive sins, like seething hatred or bestiality, which represent God's near-desperate deployment of resuscitative paddles in last-ditch efforts from Heaven to salvage man from his fatally sinful slumber. As one person may seemingly get the best of another in argument, persuasion, or deception, God sees to it that each person has the chance to know of his or her own wrongness—utter and unmistakable wrongness. Verses 24-32 set out God's relentless commitment to reveal each man to himself and each woman to herself and to offer restoration to purity and understanding.

Amidst the foolishness, coldness, darkness, futility, and the forsaking of the Almighty, God gives men over to the "sinful desires of their hearts." For many, as verse 24 contemplates, this results in sexual impurity (e.g., lust and masturbation) up through sexual immorality (e.g., fornication and adultery). Though this handover was designed to awaken the masses, the people generally motor along through verse 25, exchanging the truth of God for a lie (e.g., "this is okay," "everybody's doing it," "as long as it's consensual," "nobody's getting hurt," "don't take things too seriously"). As a postscript in verse 25, man winds up worshipping and serving created things rather than the Creator. It becomes easier and more commonplace to esteem movie stars, athletes, bosses, co-workers, neighbors, and the other sides of the fence than to give heed to an invisible, untouchable, "unknowable" God.

Nobody seems to follow the Bible at all, and it seems that any discerning architect or engineer would scrap projects fraught with such ever-crumbling results. Yet, for man God pulls and plays trump cards from Heaven in verses 26-27. In this effort to awaken man and save him by spiritual CPR if necessary, God gives man over to shameful lusts—lusts that should strike the conscience, shock the sensibilities, usher new awareness, and prompt a complete reconsideration of life. Of course, such lusts could include batty iPhone addictions, hourly Facebook fevers, wicked and criminal pedophilia, bizarre cross-dressing, backwards incest, lowly prostitution, and on and on. Among the examples featured in Scripture, homosexuality registers as a "shameful lust." For women and men, homosexuality among other shameful lusts activates and emerges as a near last-ditch effort by God in Heaven to awaken senses and arrest the madness of man that has long preceded any adult, homosexual activity. Those humble, cognizant, and obedient to verses 18-25 need never worry about homosexual handovers. But who adheres to verses 18-25? Thus, homosexuality and its fellow shames come as inexorable results of people first going their own ways.

Once arriving at homosexuality's doorway and entering its traps, no argument of men, configuration of science, or posturing of politics or policy will render it anything but shameful. Those with hardened hearts, deceived minds, and seared consciences may claim no shame, but there was a day before the darkening when shame initially prompted secretive contemplation, impulse, and action. Homosexuality's traps include what the Bible calls being "inflamed with lust" in verse 27. This characterization accounts for how such embarrassing, reckless, dangerous, mind-boggling, and unnatural sin could spread across the globe at catastrophic risk and cost. Another trap includes "receiving in themselves the due penalty for their perversion" in verse 27. Such penalties include simulation of characteristics of the opposite gender and becoming subject and liable to the allure of new and possibly suffocating lifestyles and susceptibilities. Such transformations plague homosexual offenders, especially those who genuinely hope and pray against homosexuality's activation in their own lives.

Since homosexual handovers from Heaven seem rarely to result in the afflicted revisiting previously ignored verses and safeguards, lives rumble downhill unless rescued by repentance and conversion or otherwise trapped and held fast by other externally mitigating sins (Proverbs 5:22) like breath-saving but soul-destroying cowardice (Revelation 21:8). Verses 28-32 outline a horrifying prognosis for those blasting through Heaven's conscience-striking roadblocks. God's signs against man manifest in depraved minds, in full-blown menus of wickedness, in a continuing obstinacy, and in the approval of those who join in the fray and do similarly. Verse 30 notes man's penchant for inventing ways of doing evil. Once homosexual and other shameful-lust gates open and man fails even to hiccup, slow, reconsider, self-evaluate, get honest, or repent, off to the never-before-seen destitution races he goes. And this is where America heads today under Blue leadership trying to legitimize and mainstream homosexuality.

Implications

The stakes hinging upon proper delineation of homosexuality's causes and parameters cannot be overstated. And perhaps the topic does not engender big, festive parties. Assuming the popular notion that only 10% of the populace inclines toward homosexuality, shall the electoral tail wag the dog in public policy? Will the vocal minority of the homosexual minority (i.e., those who are "out" and politically active) win its agenda against an indifferent majority (i.e., "straight" America) and a closeted majority of the minority (i.e., those non-confessional homosexuals wishing their homosexuality would ebb or disappear altogether)? With great shame being the first and foremost marker of homosexuality, should "tolerant" social mores simply ignore such insufferable burdens of disgrace permanently placed upon those not partaking of public celebrations and political movements of gay rights? Blue revelry over gay marriage hardly eases the pain and hopelessness of those gravely suffering beneath homosexuality's unforgiving clutches.

For instance, business mogul Malcolm Forbes supposedly lived a secretive homosexual life discovered only after his death. Tyler Clementi, the Rutgers University student victimized by his roommate's spy cam, threw himself from the George Washington Bridge to his death, presumably over the shame of his homosexual encounter being broadcast. Homosexual actor Rock Hudson appeared to be a ladies' man but was posthumously outed by his AIDS-related death and an aftermath of seedy publicity. Today, those who "come out" as homosexual are revered as courageous and pioneering. But why? Because of the great shame. So shall society cut short any meaningful acknowledgement of this underlying disrepute and instead build a platform of acceptance atop souls trapped in closets left to work out their shame as did Forbes, Clementi, and Hudson? Though clamor from the gay-rights movement combined with natural indifference from straight communities may make for a fertile environment of swift changes in homosexual policies, rights, and recognitions, would this not set adrift the vast majority of homosexuals trapped in darkness, shame, and doubt? Surely, this would not be the intent, would it? In its voracity, would the gay-rights movement care so little about closeted sufferers, who in shame simply cannot come out and who genuinely seek some sort of lever against homosexual activation? Are not the quiet and politically inactive largely those not so ready to slide down the Romans 1 verses? Are they not to be saluted and encouraged for their resistive efforts and ultra-inconvenient convictions?

Democratic processes shall continue to produce political results. Those neither homosexual nor spiritual may cast their votes along with everyone else, going with the flow as usual and surmising "equal rights for all." But what carries the day in these political realms hardly matters. The immovable Scriptural dictates will prove true and wreak havoc as outlined regardless of how people discern the issue and of what they decide to do about it. It will go as God has decreed it. So the people through referenda, the Courts through opinions, and the legislatures through enactments will continue to decide and do as they wish. They will likely never address the real issues, which are being premiered here.

In a democracy and in the Kingdom of God, nobody will force, demand, insist, or otherwise seek compulsory compliance with what spiritual awakening and understanding should voluntarily spawn. And these are not hate issues or matters resolvable by votes or opinions. These are purely spiritual and educational issues. Everyone gets to work out his or her faith, salvation, and relationship with God. However, the fervor with which advocates of homosexuality have pressed their solitary issue smacks of stories in Scripture with fire-from-Heaven endings. As an intermediate step, perhaps God would first allow willing Reds, a la Abraham, to escape the forthcoming heavenly backlash.

<u>*Conclusions*</u>

Neither birthed nor chosen, homosexuality activates at

the adverse judgment of God on the basis of other deliberate sins. Thus, homosexuality stands as a specified Romans 1 handover and nothing more or less. On the exact pathway that other sins and shames are sown and reaped, homosexuality stands indistinct and unworthy of special treatment. Where lies the "adulterer's rights" movement? What of the "prideful rights" crusades? Strangely, perhaps such odd support groups will misguidedly arise one day—in Blue States, of course. In a morally balanced society, homosexuality cannot be honored or excused above adultery, carousing, deceit, pride, or a host of other unacceptable sins. But as the current state of affairs essentially gives only a slap on the wrist for these other disgraces, homosexuality also now receives popular acceptance on the basis of moral decay but not on the basis of any enlightenment.

Ultimately, parades, causes, and political upheavals represent but a fight for crumbs. Winning the argument while still being wrong should hardly elicit any genuine celebration. In the same vein, religious denouncements and ineffective teachings which fail to unfold the Scriptures also prove counterproductive. And, let all be warned yet again to avoid adoption of convenient convictions: those positions held not on the basis of rightness but on the basis of preference.

In reality, the debate over homosexuality has generally taken place amongst a merely conveniently convicted triumvirate: the vocal and hardened homosexual offenders who want what they want; the disinterested masses who easily sway and lack a dog in the fight; and those disgusted by the shame of it all and wishing it would all go away. In any case, God will get His, man will get his, and there should remain no confusion as to the how and why of the happenings.

This chapter provides but one solitary yet stunning example of just how far askew the impassioned Blue agenda will go. There are dozens more. Dead wrong in their assumptions, Blues nonetheless pour the coal into their pet programs and causes, either because of rampant cluelessness or to steal away otherwise Red votes. Most remarkably, despite dreadful results, Blues push ever ravenously according to their bottomless whimsy. No proofs, no caution flags, and no retracement of steps mark the Blue agenda. At whatever cost, the Blues will advance blithely to the unnecessarily bitter end. As usual, against this unreasoning onslaught, escape remains the only option for the Reds while the Blues, full steam ahead, burn down their own lives.

4. A BARBARIC MAJORITY

The Declaration, the Constitution, and the founding of America assumed an informed, hard-working, autonomy-loving citizenry. Its framers had gleaned from history and had learned firsthand that dictatorships deprive people of liberty and that true democracies tend to fizzle badly from unintelligent and ignorant masses unable to make wise choices. Therefore, the United States was founded neither upon monarchy nor upon pure democracy. Like it or not, struggle with it or not, the framers knew what they were doing.

However, as America's vote spread to the masses, a country with 300 million citizens now has over 100 million receiving welfare benefits—not Social Security, not Medicare, but welfare benefits (i.e., unentitled monies, vouchers, and credits from other people). Do these 100 million people have any conscientious trouble taking from others? Not likely, as not surprisingly the core of this one-third of the populace votes almost unanimously Blue to keep its unearned benefits rolling in. The framers' concerns about democracy have become modern-day nightmares as welfare and other benefit recipients overwhelmingly vote their self-interests to the accumulating detriment of themselves (e.g., evacuated self-respect) and everyone else (e.g., burial beneath debt).

To effect such a transfer of wealth from maker to taker, the political class emerged. These blatherers brandished zero good ideas, had nothing to add or give, but rather seized upon openings afforded by a nonconversant electorate to gain office, position, power, and a lifetime on a dumb and easy street. These developments have transformed the nation, plunging it into a dizzyingly relentless electoral frenzy. Leadership has become a thing of the past in America. Everything comes affixed to political calculation and couching. And as nobody leads, America bleeds. And in the end, no matter their history, promise, or supposed destiny, those suffering unstoppable bleeding will ultimately perish. This has become America at this present hour, and it represents her undoing by constitutional hijackers and their silly supporters with the collective viewpoints of a June bug.

Though America was never perfect, her remarkably lively and sentient founding supplied a wisdom and a way for sovereign people to remain self-directing, for progress to be pioneered, for rights and responsibilities to endure, and for future generations to reach their potentials and taste individual opportunities. But the tiny ideas of petite men, as they usually do, reduced to rubble the dreams of exalted men while the supposed caretakers slept at the wheel. The damage runs so deep at this point that America cannot possibly retrace her missteps. Rather, first and foremost, she must painfully come apart. The current, omnipresent rattling and rumbling represent only the beginnings of indispensible disintegration.

Here, proven once again, prevailingly passive, uncultivated, and self-seeking lives and thoughts undo democracies every time. Such me-first factions of civilizations always sell themselves to preying bidders and then woefully spend the remainder of their days boohooing and paying for their haste.

At this juncture, though no more time exists for uncertainty, President Obama continues to reign as Uncertainty-in-Chief. Though the clocks indicate an expiration of time for argument, the irrelevant, small-scale fiscal debates rage, one after another after another. And though delay cannot be afforded, it appears that only sometime around never will the topic of federal *spending* ever reach the agenda. Though the majority of the people do not understand enough to care or act, the tick-tock expiration looms and daily weighs heavily upon those paying any attention.

America's federal government has so completely and immorally squandered all of its conscripted wealth that not a single dollar remains to conduct the government, fund the military, support a safety net, or cover any other operating expense. In the 2012 fiscal year, the foolish feds collected \$2.5 trillion in taxes, fees, and other revenues, and then spent all of it on entitlement payments (\$2.3 trillion) and interest` on the debt (\$0.2 trillion), which currently prices at temporary, rock-bottom rates. With zero dollars left over, the "masterminding" feds borrowed an additional \$1.3 trillion and spent all of it running the government, fighting wars, and distributing welfare benefits. Horrifyingly, this represents the past, present, and future blueprint of each of the Obama years. Repeating, in the event the first go-round was so outlandish as to be dismissed as fantasy: without ever spending a dime to fund the government or to protect the nation, the feds found themselves penniless after collecting and squandering $2.5 trillion and then unconscionably borrowed every dollar required to execute the only duties the government was designed to fulfill in the first place. Brilliant!

Far beyond the ruthless dismantling of America, the Blue majority has now pressed onward with a downright barbaric course, applauded and/or tolerated by most. Partial-birth abortion (the equivalent of infanticide), special homosexual protections and sensitivities, and embryonic stem-cell research using taxpayer dollars represent a few of the outlandish practices birthed in the Obama years. Enmeshed in the driver's seat for the rest of 50-state America's future, Blues have driven the country into its most overtly barbaric seasons, almost as if to test whether anyone anymore cares.

The Hunger Games

America has weaned itself from God, de-emphasized charity, and set out to nestle at the counterfeit bosom of government. Those striving to live up to being made in God's image easily notice these monstrous developments. God also notices. Exploitative politicians do not care. And the dopey masses seem forever enamored of the ignoble goal of merely logging another pointless and temporary day into the books. Honestly, the results already resemble a landscape of horrors.

The Hunger Games, best-selling novel and top-drawing motion picture, depicts a futuristic society where flamboyantly oblivious and wayward elites run a world in which adolescents conscripted by lottery compete to the death for the sheer entertainment of others. The portrayed masses are pacified by their own superficial rooting interests, while the elite remain amusedly self-absorbed and unchallenged despite their despicable weirdnesses. American audiences in 2012 were both mesmerized and aghast at these images. "Fiction," most would figure. However, *The Hunger Games* literally becoming American reality represents no stretch at all for the morally vacant barbarians who have already crash-landed and ruined America!

The homosexual detour and its populist movement discussed in the previous chapter exemplify a road of perverse disregard and resultant depravity. America has been hurtling down that slippery highway across many controversies at great velocity for many years now. Nothing in *The Hunger Games* shocks any more greatly than does America's 2013 diminishing course already well under way. Those who profess otherwise have either been asleep or have had their consciences seared so as not to notice or care, as proclaimed Scripturally in 1 Timothy 4:2.

Now, even free speech and expression are attacked and censured. For example, to appease fickle and financially hypersensitive sponsors, radio talk-show host Rush Limbaugh apologized for referring to Georgetown Law student Sandra Fluke as a "slut." Fluke had testified before Congress of the need for giveaway contraceptives amidst the controversy as to whether Catholic churches and other employers were required to provide contraceptives through insurance plans pursuant to Obamacare edicts. In any case, Limbaugh's outburst against Fluke only served to make her a household name, and his "apology" once again left the philistines of society feeling justified and triumphant. Consequently, there was

Fluke with a prime-time speaking role at the Democratic National Convention, clamoring for contraceptives and rights to abort and on and on. Seriously? What seaworthy evidence really exists to dispute that *The Hunger Games* have arrived already? While the world wages war, natural disasters tear asunder, financial sins catch and tackle populations, and civilizations' futures hang in the balance, Fluke and her ilk clamor for contraceptives funded by others and for the green light to kill unborn babies if somehow still conceived? How does this scenario not embarrass these savages? But with Fluke and her kind, all such sensitivity and objectivity has been long lost. Apparently, nothing enthralls or arouses the passions like baby's blood.

As if abortion were not uncivilized enough, stem-cell harvests from fetal farming further lowers the bar of unseemliness to new, villainous depths. Back in more honorable days, humble and reverent hearts and minds accepted fates falling from Heaven. Today, child parts are refrigerated and then loudly and joyfully harvested when some trouble befalls the greedy and mercilessly hardened. Maladies should not require murderous and dismembering rectifications, should they? Today, as long ago unequivocally rebuked, man invents and undertakes a menu of evils that never even entered God's vast and creative mind (Jeremiah 7:31).

Alarmingly, Blue proponents follow paths similar to those taken by leaders, facilitators, and operatives in *The Hunger Games.* For example, both groups remain straight-faced and strident when they should be blushing over their outlandish behavior. For example, though teetering on conscience and embarrassment for a brief moment, Los Angeles mayor Antonio Villaraigosa finally went ahead and dutifully read his teleprompter lines to stick

"God" and "Jerusalem" back into the 2012 Democratic National Convention platform despite an obvious lack of legitimate bases or delegate support. Of course, excision of "God" and "Jerusalem" from the platform in the first place largely went unexplained, unaccounted for, and relegated as no big deal. Reversing course, as Villaraigosa so forced, was clearly aimed at saving face in public relations. Such shenanigans mixed with blankness of expression marks and drives implementation of Blue ideology. No matter the shocking developments in *The Hunger Games* or in Blue battle cries, the straight, disaffected expressions (other than seething anger and/or limp-wristed flamboyance) evince a death of conscience and of soul. Whereas lack of sensitivity and practicality formerly marked causes for concern, Blue ideas and policies have blown well past those historical speed bumps and warning signs.

Entertainment formerly offered well-timed or well-deserved breaks from the ordinary. Now, entertainment has become the ordinary. The modern world formerly gasped at the horrors of ancient times. The Roman Colosseum marks a time of morally vacant, deathly entertainment. Today's rah-rah, gay-gay, abort, gimme, stem-cell, down-with-God, cannot-blush, amuse-me, Blue narrative, supported by enough people and leaders to be here to stay, shows that the Colosseum could easily re-open for business without any additional stretch of Blue moral rules. Tolerance, appeasement, fear, and hoping it will go away have failed to rebuff *The Hunger Games* tsunami from becoming a new and terrifying American reality.

The fact that Blues will overreact to this assessment and ostentatiously protest in their familiar noisemaking only further substantiates the foregoing and buttresses the requirement that Reds bypass Blues to avoid a *Hunger Games* finish. Blah blah to the Blues. Their noises only prove true the premises of this entire work. They will not be able to help themselves from confirming every facet of this essay to be tragically true. Ultimately, incorrigible sodomites and their staunch backers—together sporting deadpan, amoral looks and cheering murderous policies—make for one oversized, moronic party for the stupefyingly selfish. This hardly seems like a crowd with which a nation of any longevity or promise could be built. Surely, it seems much more like a movie of horrors come true!

Three Roots

In the overall scheme of things, support for President Obama and Blue ideology stems from three possible roots: low intelligence, ignorance, and/or problems with God. And these three roots are most often manifested across various forms of simpleness, selfishness, animalism, insecurity, and the like. While Reds are hardly immune from low intelligence, ignorance, or problems with God, of Red and Blue only Red ideology can ever be squared with the Declaration, the Constitution, and the Bible.

The issue of healthcare in America well showcases these three roots of America's barbaric majority. Surely, low intelligence and/or ignorance are prerequisites to thinking American healthcare can be afforded for all by government decree. And problems with God form the cornerstone of America's inability to tame the healthcare behemoth. Shockingly, the majority has become so blinded that it cannot see any of these roots, in healthcare or elsewhere. Illuminating, the healthcare topic warrants further discussion here.

The Obama administration and its short-lived supermajority in Congress pressed hard and ultimately refashioned the healthcare system in the United States in 2009 and 2010. Much of the reform's argument centered upon the supposed 50 million uninsured people in the country and adopted precedent support from the socialized European and Canadian healthcare systems. Yet, healthcare at its most advanced and sophisticated levels as developed in the United States simply cannot be afforded by all or for all. This assertion steeped in financial and moral reality hardly represents a crime or an offense. Citizens routinely go without items of far greater value than healthcare (e.g., good parenting, spiritual insight, personal responsibility). And in any event, no sensible society should ever divorce individual healthcare burdens from individual healthcare-related willingness and effort to care for self. Seriously, everyone must pay bills associated with another's decision to smoke? Overeat? Self-mutilate? Drink? Obsess? Hate?

Unfortunately, for this barbaric society bent on what it wants and not on what is right, two cardinal rules in healthcare will seemingly never reach the Congressional floor for discussion or the considerate desk of a president for signature. These rules confound the unintelligent, escape the ignorant, and skewer the godless. Thus, they completely bowl over America without Americans even knowing what hit them. Rule number one: *spiritual problems cannot be medicated.* Rule number two: *God will not contend with man forever.* To its demise, the entirety of the healthcare debate, along with its legislative and judicial tumult, has completely overlooked these two immovable edicts.

Concerning the first rule—that spiritual problems cannot be medicated—the Scriptures, replete with examples, teach that people are almost always going astray and coming up with their own bright ideas to cater to their very own wish lists, regardless of what God has to say about it. For example, without an actual saving relationship with God, all are destined for great anxiety and trouble. The Deuteronomy 28:64-68 verses seem quite biographical for human populations, which struggle mightily as prophesied. In addition, God has also sown everyone in weakness, which was supposed to be delightfully understood and endured (1 Corinthians 15:43 and 2 Corinthians 12:10). But rather than humble themselves before a faithful Creator and commit to His direction, people seek medicines, among other equally impotent options. In this, the people attempt to reverse things like how God has made them (e.g., in weakness) and how God lets people know that they stand distant from Him (e.g., via anxiety). America's incredible healthcare system has failed because it is misused to shield the people from God's interactive advances. The United States has thereby deeply plunged itself into this incredibly messy and pricey marsh bereft of solution because its cures are spiritual and not medical. The popular chorus demands payment of outrageous medical expenses that ironically stem from untreated spiritual deficits. These costs can never be paid unless people legitimately turn to God en masse, reverse their deliberate spiritual transgressions, and relinquish their selfish insistences.

Medicating *spiritual* problems is sinful and bankrupting. This issue screams out in the healthcare debate, yet nobody hears it or echoes it. The readily perceptible matter of people paying through the nose trying to medicate God's wrath has not been broached at any time during debates over healthcare. This shameful and inexcusable blindness will serve as God's sign to the people that they have ignored Him yet again.

Turning to the second rule—that God will not contend with Man forever—no matter how much money is taxed, printed, borrowed, or otherwise gotten, it will never be enough to outspend God's declaration, "My Spirit will not contend with man forever, for he is mortal…" (Genesis 6:3). People must die, for God has decreed it. People must cease looking to man to reverse God's irreversible ruling as if it were an outdated legislative act or a reviewable opinion from some lower tribunal.

People have no doubt become enamored of the notion that the life to live is the one on Earth and that that "life" can last longer and longer and longer. However, there remains absolutely no way to fund cutting-edge healthcare for America's ever-aging population, though apparently nobody but God dares to say as much. For, as God did at the Tower of Babel (Genesis 11:1-9), He has confounded those insistent upon lengthening earthly lives without authority from Heaven. Accordingly, God has brutally frustrated America's entire healthcare system. Of course, repentance stands as the only solution to these two rules. But nobody should hold his or her breath because repentance never gets elected.

The unintelligent, ignorant, and godless would seem to have much work to do. But humility, education, and repentance could turn things around instantaneously. Neither a healthcare system nor any other program designed to shortcut real solutions to these three root problems shall ever prevail. God will maintain His relationship with His individuals. And, as outlined in the next chapter, God has demonstrated His great displeasure toward Blue generalizations of people, as each heart and life totes individual dictates that cannot be ignored, infringed, or denied.

Blue Misery

As Reds find themselves generally busy living ambitious and meaningful lives, they too often think the best of others who have long proven to be nonsensical. California Congresswoman and House Minority Leader Nancy Pelosi? Seriously? Three words: "Nancy," "Pelosi," and "Really?" What are the Reds waiting for? Have they been hypnotized? Lost their compasses? Forsaken their standards? Succumbed to the wacky Blue narratives of life? Have they become those proverbial elephants spoofed in infancy by link chains that psychologically seem insurmountable even in adulthood?

Nevada Senator and Senate Majority Leader Harry Reid? President Barack Obama? Seriously? Let the Blues have them since they love them so. The Reds must waste zero words and zero seconds on the stupidity of a world where the words and ideas of Pelosi, Reid, and Obama are taken seriously at all, ever. These three have proven, down to each of their uttered syllables, that only contemptible and empty thoughts and musings lie in their wells. Who in his or her right mind would ever tolerate a world where the minds of Pelosi, Reid, and Obama register and count, let alone where they coldly strafe and bulldoze 300 million lives?

The lazy, grabby world gets worked up over

nothingness, for it has nothing else to do. But free people are radically different. They relish having an entire world to explore, lives to live, dreams to fulfill, and plans to execute. Let the bothered vent to the fence post or to the traffic light or to the wall. Let the Reds get on with life already. This long, drawn-out tango must be brought to a merciful conclusion. Fighting and losing a civil war would be preferable to the tyranny of having to engage the Blues in conversation over matters of freedom, civility, and destiny. Let the Blues work their voodoo upon their own. Let the Reds prove the wisdom of independence. No sober person could ever tolerate or put up with the Blues. They have been given over to madness, and they love it that way. For instance, how can programs be developed, promulgated, and instituted without due regard to funding? For the Blues, cheers stream from the mere mention of spending and giving and sprawling and pouring. Apparently, it never occurs to any of them that the flip side of such celebrations involves someone paying for them. No wonder Blues drive all of their economies into the ground. Not even wild beasts do this. But there is no slowing the Blues. The Reds must act boldly or resign themselves to compulsory lives on the Tilt-a-Whirl: nausea, vomiting, and listlessness for everyone.

Seriously, what kind of meaningful conversation can anyone expect to have with those who protest chickens being deprived access to proper yards but boisterously applaud and furiously demand green lights to butcher unborn children upon any whimsical basis and to farm out their parts as the latest and greatest bandages? With straight faces, how can expecting Blue moms and dads rejoice at movements in the womb on one hand but then wholeheartedly and shamelessly support abortion on the other? Answer: a voluntary hardening of heart that should have alarmed and awakened them to the ills and evils of Blue ideology. But, as has been painfully learned around the world for hundreds of years, waking from a moral slumber has hardly been a Blue specialty.

In reality, Blue rabidity ironically and largely stems from deep-seated insecurity. The Blues know in their recessed consciences that they are morally wrong about a great many things. On one hand they will voraciously enact legislation protecting grasslands and projected walkways for eventually hatching turtles. Yet on the other hand they loudly and defiantly back murder in cases of failed abortions lest any "mother" have to suffer knowing that a child of hers exists somewhere upon the Earth. Since consciences cannot square these two positions, consciences must be suppressed and obliterated. Resultant insecurities drive and hype the zeal and fervor with which Blues defend and applaud morally corrupt positions. Abortion rights will always get the greatest applause from Blues not because these rights pertain to any paramount issue but because they touch upon the greatest of insecurities (i.e., known moral wrongness). The vehemence is designed to repel the discussion altogether to avoid inwardly sunken feelings of moral decay. Similarly, anti-God sentiments like removal of Christian symbols from public lands, and morally vacant tacks like the clandestine buying of votes with welfare benefits will always receive staunch defense not because these positions matter prominently but because consciences long ago obliterated might otherwise attempt an unacceptable comeback in the hearts and minds of the Blues.

The foregoing represents but a small, bitter sampling of Blue misery. Unreasoning and incurable short of spiritual conversion, it has surely whipped itself into an irreversible frenzy in this new millennium. And it bountifully sources the nation's barbaric steps.

5. THE MUDDLE TO THE MIDDLE

The United States emerged among all nations as the freest, smartest, most moral, most favored, and most prosperous. Now of course, 44 years *after* landing on the moon, it cannot even get itself to its own space station without a lift from lesser nations. Now, its educational system focuses upon closing achievement gaps between racial groups rather than unleashing scholars upon leading, cutting, and innovative edges. Odd ethical notions of widespread, mandated equality have carpet-bombed the country, thereby dropping high standards to a more customary and unsatisfying muddle. These social-engineering agendas never work because they fly in the face of God, impermissibly narrow complex lives, and place obscene weights and harnesses upon the country's risk-takers, pioneers, and high-flyers. And for what?

Blues seem ever eager to draw lines and work within narrow, average parameters. Setting quotas, parceling out financial pie pieces, and spending lifetimes tweaking an average system seem to be a mere sampling of Blue jollies. Yet free people draw no lines, believing instead that *everything* should remain possible. Reds must snap themselves out of the muddles of America and get on with their God-given immunities and limitless possibilities.

Surrounded by muddled American political partisanship in which Republicans and Democrats hold various majorities and powers, a clear demonstration of what actually works can scarcely be shown to the masses. Pet agendas, distortions, lies, and spin prevent many citizen voters from understanding how the economy, finance, morality, and the body politic actually work. For many, good ideas have become difficult to distinguish from bad ideas. Success and failure and the causes of each have become points of endless contention and dispute. And this presents exactly the muddle that Blues love because it keeps the game to nowhere going and going and going.

But now, in education especially, real people are exiting the muddle. For instance, authentic parents are more and more utilizing virtual technologies and homeschooling their children, or enrolling their children into any number of today's proliferating charter schools. Eventually, those regular K-12 public schools being left behind will sink further as they suffer a large-scale exodus of their brightest students. Public schools and the feeble governments that operate them will become mere baby-sitting centers for un-parented kids who cannot or will not learn independently, and who will no longer have the benefit of a genuine atmosphere of education. Which of the wrongheaded social engineers will step forth and accept responsibility for the messy aftermath of this inevitability? Regardless, high achievers will more and more bid adieu to the muddled middle championed by the Blues.

Counting People Collectively

The entirety of the muddled middle stems from a failure to regard people as unique individuals. Reds so regard the people. Blues see people much more as they see cattle or cantaloupes—in crowds or piles. The Bible, the Declaration, and the Constitution all agree: The Blues are dead wrong in this.

The overwhelmingly vast majority of the world's population lives with a collectivist ideology and outlook whereby communal cares and causes trump freethinking independence. This collectivist world has accepted big lies. It has broken off the fact that God creates each person singularly, apportioning gifts and weaknesses and fashioning unique callings and expectations. The mass shrugging of these divinely effected attributes and parameters has brought wrath and curse from Heaven and has predictably spawned boredom, laziness, simplicity, neediness, and moral collapse. These reaped maladies from sown communal fabrications have then only irrationally prompted the cursed to rail against the blessed and to demand that more be given to the cursed from the blessed even as the cursed could readily change and get all they seek and more from Heaven. Not to be outwitted, immutable rules from the Almighty require that what is sown be reaped (Galatians 6:7), so the taxing and taking, no matter the upward fever pitch of it, never solves the troubles of those in want because the actual solution would be for each person to return to square one and wear the yoke and responsibility uniquely marked out for him or her. To the end of everybody's days God will tolerate no circumvention on this, no matter how many yield to the big lies and to the degradations of collectivism.

Not without grave shortcomings (e.g., slavery), the inception of the United States was nonetheless marvelously built upon the dogged protections of individuals unlike any nation in human history. Smart and ambitious men masterminded a country and its documents that would celebrate, honor, and defend the rights of individuals, and individuals only. This notion, in line with the Scriptures, found unprecedented favor from Heaven and unleashed human potential and capital that will forever be the envy of the rest of the world.

However, the disease of collectivism eventually capitalized upon two phenomena in America. First, as previously outlined, the vote in the United States was massively extended to the unknowing, to the fearful, and to the selfish through a series of constitutional amendments. Second, seedy politicians found that they could exploit the simpleness, the fear, and the greed of new voters and thereby get into office without having to be smart, virtuous, or pioneering. Finally, by 2012, the amalgamation of thoughtless, fearful, and self-seeking voters in the United States exceeded the receding number of informed, courageous, and selfless voters. Thus the United States has crossed a tipping point and shall be in decline to its projected doom unless Red States secede immediately and build remnant nations of *individuals* who not only say but actually believe and live adages promoting liberty even over life when and where a choice must be made.

The collectivist agenda gained steam by chipping away the idea of America in the 1900s. First, the advent of Social Security and Medicare might have worked as helpful supplements had the government not preemptively and criminally spent the payroll taxes collected. But, as has long been established, everything the government touches largely goes "poof." Now, the programs represent insufferable, unfunded liabilities coming due. Second, courts then developed protected *classes* of people beyond the Constitution's circumscribed *individual* protections. As a result, these special treatments initially based on race and gender will only continue to undermine the nation's individualistic precepts in favor of the world's herd-like model by which everyone is assumed to be the same.

The rest of the world lives communally perhaps because it has never seen or experienced true liberty. It knows no better. But the American system was finely designed to allow the one God loves—the cheerful giver (2 Corinthians 9:7)—to share and shepherd not because he must but because he is willing (1 Peter 5:2). Such a voluntarily and truly charitable society operates far superiorly to any competitor. Ask those of requisite age whether collegiality and genuine goodwill toward fellow man was better before or after the advent of a government robbing its citizens to fund a tidal wave of welfare.

Case in point, frightening tornadic winds tore through the town of Joplin, Missouri in 2011. Banana-republic President Obama hustled out there to reassure residents that the US Government would be there to rebuild everything. Interestingly, back in the day, President Reagan had said that the scariest words in the English language were those uttered by government employees professing to "help." How times have changed. Of course, Obama seems naïve to the notion of insurance, charity, neighbor helping neighbor, and the way in which noble human civilizations have endured and survived disasters at the finger of God from time immemorial. Vigorous mobilization of Joplin residents, contractual payouts from State Farm, a generous and charitable outpouring facilitated by The Red Cross, and assistance from other well-meaning people and entities could and would readily restore Joplin. Obama need not borrow money from China to do what actual people living like actual people can much better accomplish on their own. Of course, for the same reasons, George W. Bush going to New Orleans after Hurricane Katrina and vowing to rebuild that sub-sea-level city seemed neither reasonable nor sensible, either. It all rings of a strumming for popularity. But actual leadership would summon reasoning people to take hold of the bright idea to build upon lands well above the water table and to make proper preparations against risks. People will always rebuild what they care about. Government generally steals, borrows, and spends on whatever garners re-election. No thanks.

Heart and volunteerism characterize authentic aid and assistance. This must never be crowded out by coerced giving or by depletion of resources to the point that givers, having already been defunded by and for government largesse, have nothing left to give. Blues remain too shallow to realize that government intrusion coldly removes empathy and love, the key ingredients to giving. Thus jettisoned, affectionate camaraderie gives way to robotic, arms-length doling where inefficiencies waste, dependencies grow, and heart and soul dissolve from the scene.

Social Engineering

Because collectivism always severely underperforms its

promises, Blues always immediately take to social engineering to try to force the results they had expected and pledged. Of course, this force-fit only exacerbates the problems and never ever works, either.

The Blues fiercely refuse to understand, let alone honor, self-determination. No more breath should be expended explaining it any further. Rather, let the Blues watch and learn, if they wish. Meanwhile, Red States must proceed to live under liberating principles, which acknowledge that overcoming troubles and bearing burdens rightly constitute part of individual human destinies. In the face of obstacles, struggles, and setbacks, freedom makes perseverance commonplace and triumph possible. Insisting that everyone stop the show and pony up some bucks and some years in order to pay off these individually earmarked battles only serves to rob others of their birthrights, distract eyes from their proper targets, slow a country from its potential, and weigh down a people with incalculable hindrances.

In addition, separating individuals from their lots from Heaven and divorcing their harvests from what they have sown only serve to rile God's wrath in Heaven, for these actions break His rules and wear down a populace that can never possibly pay the unpredictable freight of such policies. The welfare state can never match the spiritual and charitable state. America flourished when it was the latter. It has begun imploding trying to become the former.

When society attempts to weigh, measure, and unriddle the calculus of an individual's troubles, society's wheels fly from their axles. For example, how do dyslexia, childhood polio, herniated intervertebral discs, orphanhood, and subjection to molestation compare to each other and compare to any of the other adversities in lives across the landscape of humanity? Seriously, as a matter of policy shall society embark upon engineering fixes for such incalculable misfortunes? Does it not make infinitely more sense for society to engender and expect common, sober understanding that any number of things can and will befall each person at some point? Should not individuals be called to insure themselves as responsible adults or to shoulder the consequences as each has his own cross to bear, at least to some meaningful degree? Should not those who roll the dice acknowledge and understand that they have chosen to stand at God's mercy but not at their neighbor's bank should they suffer loss? Elsewhere, should not society operate unburdened by crushing taxes, overwhelming and relentless regulations, and constant interference to effectuate outdated rules put in place by chronically wee-thinking politicians? If anyone gets the "bad luck of the draw" in life, is not his claim against God and not against his neighbor? And consulted for a change, would not God and His word speak to those getting the supposed bad draw and work them through it if they were only willing to see things as they actually are rather than as they are being imagined?

Red-State nations must unwind America's 2013 socially engineered pretzels. They will have their dutiful chance to deal with these and other underlying issues honestly and soberly. For example, not at all dog-eat-dog, Red States shall first recognize the efficacy of strong domestic industries. Further, leaders of Red States must be keenly aware of the severe bureaucratic hangover that will befall their citizenry even upon its release from Blue captivity. In addition, the people will suffer withdrawals from being accustomed to the lulling ways of America's past 70 years. Much emphasis and vision must be placed on developing a burgeoning and self-sustaining domestic economy rather than one built upon cheap trinkets from abroad imported to keep masses distracted and "happy" despite having but shoestring budgets either funded by taxes or destroyed by taxes.

Red States must prepare their citizens for freedom. State constitutions must be taught to children in schools and to adults in public discourse. No more shall non-stop election cycles rule the roost and play to an unrecognizably simplified people. Craziness, waste, delay, and infighting must be a thing of the past. Only genuine choices must be offered. And participation in fragile democracies must be stressed, expected, and rewarded. Two detoxifying suggestions along those lines follow.

First, citizens on public assistance shall forfeit their rights to vote. This prophylactic move must wisely and boldly be placed into Red-State constitutions. Red States will not tolerate a permanent underclass supporting a political class as happens in America in 2013. For example, President Obama's policies have been dreadful for the poor in the United States. But those same poor and especially minorities have voted hugely for him in 2008 and even more so in 2012 because he gives them things (e.g., monetary benefits and lip service). This destructive, non-self-respecting dynamic cannot obtain in seceding Red States. These new nations must do everyone a favor and not reduce the people into nameless, faceless, and hopeless votes for sale.

Removal of voting rights for those on public assistance shall keep Red States from being burdened and destroyed by debilitating self-interests controlling elections. Rather, elections must represent citizen decisions on the battle of ideas and the menu of directions as in the days of yore when leaders actually posited novel and impressive ideas rather than mere promises.

Second, parents who fail to care for their children shall be guilty of child neglect and shall thereby also forfeit their voting rights. They shall also face jail time and/or voluntary sterilization for the crime of neglect, so that no additional children should have to endure such vacuous parenting. These policies would reverse and remove current financial incentives of many to have children to receive heftier government checks. They would also require adult human beings to act like adult human beings or face appropriate consequences.

In Red nations, liberty and responsibility, hand in hand, will remove any need for America's socially engineered society currently on life support. Thereafter, Reds will easily escape the muddle to the middle, and real lives with real blood flows will re-emerge upon the American scene.

Meat Hooks

In the dark, dour film *Daybreakers*, vampires running low on the red stuff as usual begin to farm humans for their blood, keeping human victims alive and transfusing them regularly and routinely. These methods made for greater and more reliable blood supplies. Very similarly and for the longest time, Blues have unscrupulously enjoyed life on the Reds via the meat hooks by which they have subdued the Reds. Parasitic victims never had it so bad! Draining time, attention, and resources from Reds, the Blues have built an overwhelming society of entitlement and political power commensurate with a grand-scale doling of gifts to those who would vote their overweening self-interests to keep the meat hooks discriminatingly affixed. Given the historically vast resources of the United States' vibrant market economy and workforce, these meat hooks have worked for the Blues and have long-seemed to the Reds like a simple cost of doing business in America. Finally, with the fed-up hand of God and with the changing economy and demographics, the meat-hook scheme stopped working as tax revenues could no longer keep pace with overpriced entitlements. In short order, the borrowing to supplement the relatively reduced tax receipts scooted the nation to an incomprehensible debt crisis in the Obama years. Now, America cannot so easily tax any more and cannot so easily borrow any more, although the Blues happily, smugly, and robotically call for both in perpetuity.

The Blues have killed the golden goose of American opportunism with their meat hooks. World-record ingenuity, heart, charity, prosperity, and limitless opportunity proved to be not nearly enough for Blues' insatiable appetites, generation after generation after generation. And yet, still there is no sign of blushing, reconsidering, or repenting. And make no mistake, the GOP has also been a disaster and stands as no answer or solution to the sea of America's problems. The GOP meekly and apologetically meanders and panders. There is zero need of the GOP going forward.

Today, as can painfully be seen across the country and around the world, this muddle of averageness absolutely comes to nothing. The current financial crises require substantial time and proper policies to be healed, cured, and straightened, but no luxury of the requisite time exists. And buffeted by muddling half-truths from partisan mumblers at every turn, time marches to the beat of only negative progress. And any Red jostling only necessitates Blues repositioning their hooks. Escaping the hooks altogether has become the only solution to this tragically weird dynamic between Red and Blue.

Currently, states cannot effectuate the 10th Amendment or turn loose innumerable trial balloons of innovative ideas and options to see what works best for free people in the 21st century. Even for those longing to get on with life, demonstrably excellent ideas cannot be implemented. Blue States fail to notice or learn. Formerly unbridled people now suffer under the thumb of the indecisive, the non-committal, and the perpetually mooching.

States cannot enjoy their own status as world economies with distinctly fluid credit ratings. They cannot fully open for business, wheel and deal, demonstrate competence, excellence, honor, and reliability because the feds will sue them, tax them, and hound them to no end. In this way, states flail beneath a bloated, bloviating, suffocating, irresponsible, and neglectful federal parent. Therefore, open markets cannot really test and reveal the quality of state decisions and policies, and therefore states with smaller and more manageable populations still cannot become masters of their own fates. They cannot nimbly adapt and thrive. They remain stuck in a muddle with the Blues.

Time, energy, money, talent, peace of mind, and everything else are needlessly expended on the inanity of the deafening echoes of American politics still on reprehensible display in 2013. Only the Blues, who live for this drama, should anymore have to endure it. Those with real lives have an infinite number of better things to do. But make no mistake, the Blues' gravitational pull away from freedom never relents. Like any disturbing Ponzi scheme or other voracious appetite, the game must go on and on for it to pay for its past deceptions.

Like leeches, Blues eat up and live on what their meat-hook tentacles can grab and bite. There is always something new and sinister brewing in Blue Land because this *is* life to them. Another bad program, more myopic ideas, greater ways to take, and on and on march the Blues ad infinitum to the delight of the detached. Throughout US history, Blues have been rolling up the nation piece by piece. Like vampires, they can only survive if they maintain access to those with blood in their veins: real people. The Blue agenda bites, sucks, drains, discards, hunts, and repeats itself over and over again. Welcome to Blue World. Families, time, hard work, education, dreams, and a host of other valuable resources and potentials lie in Blue wakes. And again, for what?

Why in the world would anyone negotiate with Obama, his rabid followers, or the Blues any longer? Only a group as detached, anemic, and blind as the GOP would ever tolerate such fruitless interactions. Be aware, while the Blues thrive in grubbing schemes, the GOP positively shirks its purpose by playing along as some passive, insecure, and cowardly victim. Why would anyone with even the slightest clue look to either of these establishments for solutions, guidance, or anything other than the same old pointlessness for yet another 100 years?

The Blues need the Reds to make the results look average—the "happy medium" or muddle to the middle. But settling for this average outcome is actually worse than total defeat for a people granted every favor ever known to mankind.

Of course, Blues live by premises requiring that fixed

pies be equitably split, while Reds operate under assumptions of innovation and the notion that pies may forever be enlarged so that all may benefit, prosper, and thrive without bounds. Left alone, the absurdity of the Blues will sink them into the abyss. They will need bailout after bailout from others. At what point will the Blues yield to superior ideas? Never, it appears. Reds must shake the dust and never again be subject to the dehumanization, the social engineering, the meat hooks, or the muddle. And freedom itself will always prevail in any fully waged battle, for God will forever be on its side.

6. DASHED DREAMS

The preamble to the Constitution declares its purposes thus: "... In Order to form a more perfect Union, establish Justice, insure domestic Tranquility, provide for the common defence, promote the general Welfare, and secure the Blessings of Liberty to ourselves and our Posterity, [we] do ordain and establish this Constitution..." Sadly, tragic norms have newly emerged since these words dried upon the parchment. As a much lesser Union, with a jumbled justice, upon a rolling domestic boil, under general retrenchments, with excessively unsecured debts, and dangling a forsaken posterity, the explicit purposes of the Constitution other than the common defense now go unfulfilled in these latter years. Dreams have been dashed in the country built of dreams!

Politically and governmentally, America has seen many grand and inspiring ideas and assurances bite the dust. National unity formerly assimilated the fiercest entity in human history. Now, unity lies well beyond national reach. Posterity used to gird Americans with the honorable notion of leaving the country in better shape for future generations. Today, this generation has completely squandered the next generation's resources, options, and potentials. The prospect of a federal balanced budget amendment nearly became reality in 1995, but has since drifted so far out of sight as to be a mere fantasy going forward. The Flat Tax and the Fair Tax have been proffered on occasion to replace the unworkable U.S. Tax Code, but American "leaders" seem to prefer the taxing labyrinth and all of its exhaustions. And President Clinton announcing that "the era of big government is over" seemed to indicate that Americans would first and foremost become responsible and then enjoy the fruits of freedom. Of course, government has only multiplied incoherently since. These moments of hope and reason apparently arose upon the horizon only to be shot out of the sky and dropped to the ground. At this point, who retains anything near the masochistic streak necessary to dare to dream again for these 50 United States?

Of the hundreds of dreams crushed by a failing America, this chapter highlights only three such despondencies. These bitter disappointments have all occurred for no good reason and show no indication of any course reversal in the future.

Tiger Cubs

What an utter disappointment and kick in the teeth that Reds now awaken in a permanently Blue America. Republican leadership since Reagan has been nothing short of atrocious. It has been hibernating at best and complicit with the Blues more commonly. And while Red citizens have been rightly busy living lives, their beloved country has been decimated while also sliding out of electoral reach. Reds had wrongly expected the Republican Party to man the store and to protect the interests of freedom and enterprise. And now, while Republicans scramble to consider feeble ways to regain a say in America, the real tragedy has become how Reds have lost their calling and their resolve to stand up for what is right. Somewhere along the way, confident, free-range, top-of-the-food-chain Reds wore down, regressed back into infancy, and abandoned their charges. Now, as mere tiger cubs—only *latently* ferocious and powerful—they hardly anymore know their own strengths or responsibilities. Now playful and altogether too accommodative of nonsense, these Reds must once again eat of the lean red meat of higher truths, regain taste for their birthrights, hear once again of their potentials, dream again of their destinies, and act again as people unwilling to cede the Earth and noble causes to the effeminate, the ludicrous, the whiny, and the wrong. This book should easily smuggle enough red meat to the Reds that they might quickly re-mature and make command decisions concerning whether they wish to surrender their lots or whether they might yet stand firm in the final national tussle between selfless and selfish, free and captive, pie makers and pie eaters.

Amidst the crushed hopes, a window of opportunity still exists for Reds to grow up again and to reestablish themselves. Even in the most divided elections in recent history, President George W. Bush won a hefty 30 states in 2000 and 31 states in 2004, despite claiming very narrow electoral and popular vote margins. Republican presidential candidate Mitt Romney managed to win 24 states in 2012 and very narrowly lost several others. These 24 to 31 Red States, not beholden to the Blue agenda of the other 19 to 26 states, can decide at any time to be done with the disaster that has become the USA. These 24 to 31 states contain a supermajority of American landmass, an undeniable though currently dormant penchant for unfettered individual liberty, and substantial natural resources, particularly in domestic energy reserves and arable land. Energy frontiers, relief from arcane federal prohibitions and stifling regulations, a plentiful supply of well-paying vocations, a market-darling status, oil pipelines, stratified opportunities, and the chance again to become the envy of the world await Reds and Red States that slap themselves awake and reemerge as 600-pound tigers and never again forget the responsibility that comes with such strength and fortune.

Should the battle appear too fierce, the road too convoluted, the move too bold or unpatriotic, curses from Heaven will fall not so much upon the Blue States where expectations and standards hover beneath the floorboards but upon the Red States where much heftier demands have been placed, for "from everyone who has been given much, much will be demanded" (Luke 12:48). At any time that Red States doubt their destinies to get on with lives of actual living, they can take courage from America's founding documents, they can soberly recall their unique calling across human history, and they can seriously consider whether they would rather continue being led on leashes held by Pelosi, Reid, and Obama.

Even pacified tiger cubs awaken for fresh, red meat. What the Red States will do remains an open question. Reds have already dashed the dreams of a generation by diminishing themselves and going along with a Blue agenda for the past 25 years and continuing. They will be tested and revealed. Most people across history wimp out, shrink back, try to save themselves, appease idiocy, hope for the best, and wait and see. Reds have been on that course for a good, long time. Now, beneath the worst American government imaginable, Reds and their states must ask themselves what in the world they are waiting for. The people of America not only instituted this contemptible tragedy of a government but have also reelected it despite its horrific record with its unabashed vacuity of coherence and intelligence. The clock has run out and the verdicts are in. Do the Reds and the Red States know who they are? The time to decide has come. There is a grand total of zero alternative routes. The questions must be asked and answered. Will the Red States escape in order to maintain the lone remaining bastion of bona-fide liberty on the planet? Or will the Red States join the rest of the compromised, low-horizoned, narrow-minded world and settle as humans whose primary goal has degenerated to one of meager survival? With some red meat on their tongues, the Red States will very soon answer those questions by way of their responsive actions. Perhaps the Reds will reverse the work of this dream-wrecking era, and render it an acerbic learning experience never to be revisited again. Until then, dreams lay shattered across the land.

The Newt Moments

Make no mistake. The only legitimate hint of Reagan's idealism and America's founding flavors since The Gipper left office after 1988 was the 2012 Republican primary candidacy of former Speaker of the House Newt

Gingrich. Newt's stunning command of history, his rapid-fire articulation of grand ideas, his unrivaled understanding of the scope of America's hurdles, and his original solutions to complex problems repeatedly set him far apart from the crowded Republican field. Lucid, rejuvenating, and fearless, Newt showed himself to be far and away the most powerful and charismatic candidate in the GOP. Twice he rose to the top of primary polling. He dominated the debates, received fitting praise and adulation for his views and oratory, and seemed to signal the possibility of a new day in America, one where a president could once again possibly be the smartest person in the room.

On the campaign trail Gingrich had posited the notions that Black Americans needed jobs rather than food stamps and that Black students would do well to be hired as janitors in their schools. In one debate exchange, Fox News contributor Juan Williams sophomorically suggested that Gingrich's ideas were "insulting to Black Americans." In response, Gingrich vigorously defended his positions, offered a soaring vision to Black Americans and all Americans, and energized the attentive crowd, which rendered its approval via standing ovations. At that inspiring and hopeful moment, the other GOP hopefuls, including eventual nominee Mitt Romney, looked their part—averagely insignificant.

In the second South Carolina primary debate, CNN's John King opened the festivities by asking Gingrich to respond to televised allegations by Gingrich's ex-wife that Newt had asked for an "open" marriage allowing them to "see" other people. Gingrich lit King up like a Christmas tree to the raucous delight of the live audience. His impassioned response again reduced the stature of his challengers by comparison and left them and their ideas in the distance. Ironically, though this line of questioning pressed directly upon Gingrich's susceptibility from having had three marriages, the alacrity of Newt's response turned a nasty knuckleball pitch into a 500-foot home-run deep into the cheap seats. Gingrich won the South Carolina primary easily and decisively. His second ascendancy in the Republican nominating tour was in hand.

Immediately thereafter, however, something wholly unacceptable happened, and any and all hope of America getting a real president or a real turnaround strategy crashed to the ground. Romney and his backers produced a deluge of unfairly negative advertising that once again spooked GOP voters and steered them away from Gingrich on the basis of one solitary fear: that Gingrich would not be able to beat President Obama in a general-election vote. Romney, the married-once and all-around nice guy, went the narrative, would better relate to and receive support from general-election voters. This scare-tactic narrative and Romney's unseemly attacks on Gingrich in the Florida debates, spelled the end of Gingrich's rise and paved the way for Romney to win based upon his financial resources and the fear with which he had pierced wimpy GOP electors. In this vein, the GOP showed itself to be worse than the Democrats and President Obama precisely because the GOP knows better but repeatedly refuses to act better whereas the Democrats and Obama have shown zero sign of possessing a clue in the first place.

After the South Carolina debates, on January 21, 2012, this author tweeted, "Newt vs. Obama, either way, changes the world in 10 months. Romney vs. Obama changes nothing, and over the cliff we all go within 20 years." How true that tweet remains. Many had dreamed of a Gingrich-Obama campaign in order that truths might actually be told and that Obama might be confronted to answer real questions and true challenges. In a presidential campaign between Gingrich and Obama, the clarity of the choice, the distinction between the competent and the Manchurian, the choice between an authentic candidate and a known pretender would have brought the race to such a boil that the country would have radically changed either way. A Gingrich win would have radically and sweepingly reduced government and driven the nation back to its roots, advocating fiscal responsibility and innovation. In a Gingrich presidency, America would have had one last hope. But even in an Obama victory over Gingrich, Newt's candidacy would have nonetheless crystallized the issues to such a stark degree that Gingrich supporters and Red States would not have dishonored their stoked dreams by accepting an Obama victory. Rather, they would have begun seceding immediately after the election. Thus, either way, that election campaign—Obama versus Gingrich—would have changed the world.

But with the GOP nomination of the moderate and easygoing Romney, none of the precipitative fireworks prerequisite to grand change could reach the sky in the 2012 election. What a shame for America, for mankind, and for real hope and change. Dreams fell to the ground once again. And now, the case that Newt would have made, which he somewhat unveiled in the primary, must be presented state by state without the benefit of the rapt attention gathered during electoral seasons.

The GOP primary electorate should once again be fully ashamed of itself. Doing anything based upon fear remains anathema before both God and man. Choosing a presidential candidate based upon fear is even worse, especially at this crippled hour in American history. Romney energized no GOP primaries during his six years running for president. His best attributes shone only when compared to Obama. But he seemed to *look* the part, and GOP voters cared so much about what non-GOP voters would think that "looks" prevailed. Sadly, the forsaken Republicans are the only people slower than the Democrats. Yes, Democratic policies are idiotic. Worse than that, the GOP embarks upon its nominating process with eyes laser focused on unwarranted and misguided concerns over what the Democrats might think about the results of that process. By the way, Blues like cookies and not Republican choices, so the GOP should just go ahead and nominate a real candidate for a change. Regrettably, it is hardly possible to get duller or more blameworthy than the GOP, which is right but too cowardly to live like it!

President Lincoln's eerie prophecy that America could only crumble from within haunts the nation 150 years later. Gingrich set out attractive themes and dreams, but subject to the assent of double-minded cowards he lost the nomination. Only a dream-come-true debate showdown between Newt Gingrich and Barack Obama *mano-a-mano*, in which Obama would have been resoundingly and intellectually eviscerated, perhaps could have effected salvation for America. That dream being dashed, along with many others, only Red exodus now remains.

Trent W. Ling

Tackling the Home Team

Usain Bolt sprints to another series of gold medals. Apple's Tim Cook unveils the cutting-edge iPhone 5. Billionaire Warren Buffet thrives into his eighties. Stage sensation *Les Miserables* comes to theaters atop remarkable talent employing a novel filmmaking approach. In none of these cases would it occur to any sane person to interfere with such lofty enterprises and efforts. Not many would tolerate a world where such ambitious and singular achievements could randomly or maliciously be discouraged or snuffed out. Rather, the living, breathing, human world rightly celebrates, applauds, and marvels at such undertakings and accomplishments. It should be this way for all, and not solely in instances involving high-profile examples. However, when the subjects of individual pursuit and progress become nameless and faceless everyday dreamers, society's penchant for simplistic communal answers interferes with ambitious movers and shakers. Truly, it is as if the Blues leap from the bushes to tackle any Reds setting out to live lives.

For example, some parents actually commit to the excellent raising of their children—juggling careers, schedules, finances, and priorities to make it all work. The goals and results are every bit as inspiring as another Bolt world record or another Buffet billion. However, lazy and superficial policies render such individual and noble decision-making all the more problematic and obstacle-laden. Exorbitant tuitions due to overwhelming governmental monetary inflows, escalating insurance rates due to lowered participation rates, and downright lending freezes due to calamitous government intrusions and systematic destruction of credit markets exact severe punishments upon good behavior that should rather be encouraged, not expunged.

Rational and moral people insure health, life, and property. Conversely, others expect and demand that society underwrite and remunerate any personal losses. Ambitious and responsible individuals contract with others to bring dreams and imaginations to fruition to the worldwide benefit of all in most cases. And yet, collective governmental policies discourage and punish such enterprises through taxation and time-consuming regulation, while simultaneously and mindlessly rewarding opposite behavior by giving money to those who have not the means to raise their own children and by giving credit forgiveness without punishment other than the slap on the wrist of a bad credit report to those who pay no regard to their creditors or their moral obligations to repay. These few examples well represent today's American government, which, though thoroughly barren of ideas and solutions, makes toxic those environments in which it injects itself.

If Blue and Red were regular individuals, and Blue brought suit against Red for some of Red's stuff, just because, a realistic court of law would toss out the case immediately. Of course, a Blue court might massage the case and use it to re-write the law, but that only further highlights Blue disease. How, in a factual scenario that Judge Wapner would scold, can Blues seek from Reds *and* insist that Reds not be allowed to get away? Those hoping or anticipating that Blues will one day come to their senses will only perish wholly unsatisfied. This is what Blues do because this is what Blues have become. The verdict is in, and future actions are predictable and projectable. Blues not only steal every resource, they steal noble dreams from hard-working others.

If not tackled by the Blues at every turn, America would flourish beyond recognition. Most poignantly, the juxtaposition of Hiroshima, Japan, and Detroit, Michigan illuminates the differences between Red and Blue policies, blessings, and outcomes. Detroit, the Motor City and one-time beacon for industry and prosperous blue-collar employment, succumbed to doltish and greedy Blue ideas and agendas. It stands today as a burned-out shell of a city for all to see and understand, even as it now goes into state receivership. Hiroshima, the first city in the world to be nuked, rose from cancerous ashes through smart and economically open avenues to shame America's Detroit. Thus, even if the Blues held the White House, nuked the Reds, and poured grand resources into Blue cities, the sharp and volitional Reds would easily eclipse the foolish and socialist Blues in a matter of years despite such diametrically reversed beginnings.

But are those Reds just trying to sneak away without sharing? No, not at all. Though the Blues do not understand it or like it, Red lives depend on autonomy and vision, and are not driven at all by money or selfishness. For example, some people may study hard, work deftly, and aim to retire early in order to enjoy their spouses, children, parents, grandchildren, friends, and neighbors. Nobly they may not intend to work to the bone for mere money until death. Selfish?

It used to be the norm for American families to forgo riches for the sake of their children by having at least one parent at home. Now, everybody seems destined to work to death and to be taxed to death, as if that course were one to look forward to or one to be proud of. Some parents actually set out to raise their children for real. They tuck them into bed in the evening, wake them for school in the morning, clothe them, feed them, keep watch over them, and pay for all of it. They attend their kids' events, concerts, ball games, and open houses. They travel with their kids and adjust to schools' seasonal calendars and prepare for grander occasions afforded by children having many consecutive days away from school. They rest as a family and enjoy a moment's peace together. These remain the rightful ambitions of bona fide parents. And yet incessant Blue interference and tackling make this model scenario more and more difficult for all, and now impossible for most.

Some, who would dare to honor aging parents, may wish to put a little aside for elderly eventualities. Some would enjoy spending extra time with their older parents, and some must make accommodations when mom and dad can no longer really take care of themselves around the clock. In a thoughtful world, grown children would spend time, money, sweat, and heart to work out their own family's unique situations, remaining always at the ready. However, today young adults are squeezed by their own careers and by the needs of their own children and parents, which represent proper and manageable burdens. Beyond that, they are crushed by governments taking from them and giving to others whether those others have shown any heart, sweat, or effort or not. The first order of business for human adults is to please God, and God will first require human adults to care for their immediate families in order to avoid being worse than unbelievers (1 Timothy 5:8). Many fail miserably in this regard and subsequently weigh down everybody else and make it hard for others to fulfill their own primary obligations. The backwardness of the Blue system violates each of these admonitions and the dreams which lie beneath them.

Some professionals would love to change gears,

having already paid their hard-working, high-level dues. Some may seek greater personal fulfillment in something relatively low-paying like teaching, writing, or volunteering. But with the bloated government and the greedy hands behind it, such transitions become economically impossible. And for that, the whole world suffers across the generations. Yet nobody wakes up. At all. Ever!

Furthermore, it has long been known and established that Reds far outpace Blues in charitable giving. Of course, no group in human history can compete with the rate at which Blues give away other peoples' money, but that does not count with God or even with thoughtful men and women. Blues need not worry so much. Anyone intent upon stinginess and tight-fistedness will get theirs—on Earth and afterward. Though the Blues seem convinced that true charity could never suffice, such conclusions stem largely from the relatively uncharitable Blue mindset itself and not at all from documented Red realities.

For those responsible citizens who pay taxes, insurances, mortgages, tuitions, debts, and charitable commitments, in addition to shelling out substantial sums for all other expenses of living in America in 2013, can they not then turn to their loved ones and friends and expend any remaining time or resources on them? Or must they essentially be robbed to pay for irresponsible citizens who not only fail to pay for their own responsibilities of life but, beyond that, need a gun-toting, steely-eyed government to come get theirs from those whose behavior, ethics, and outlook should be applauded and emulated and not tackled and embezzled against? America has collapsed mostly because it has become a morally backward place where the upright are punished and robbed, and the corrupt are rescued and rewarded. This has become a house of cards because of its repugnance. The only shocking thing here is that a meteor has not yet come from the skies to eliminate this senseless system. Fate must be leaving it up to a Red awakening and departure.

When many have become content with food, shelter, and zero work requirements, how can a society with a straight face rob the ambitious to support the lazy? Such a system is destined to crumble because of its two-fold immorality. First, tolerating, let alone fostering and rewarding, human lives content with no life cannot long remain. Second, tackling and weighing down the ambitious from destined flight cannot long persist. Such a society must burn out upon the ash heap of history as not only pathetically ineffective but morally corrupt and spiritually vacant.

But how can reversal be hastened in a world where over half of one's salary is gobbled up by various taxes and fees and then funneled away to bankroll a molasses of a government that, out of breath, exhausts itself trying to "help"? This whole Blue myopia fundamentally misses the excellent and outstanding, which increasingly cannot be afforded because American human existence has been reduced to the pathetic goal of *getting by* at the expense of *flying high*. Incalculable is the number of dreams that have fallen to the ground over this woefully cirrhotic system.

CONCLUSION

Torrentially and intestinally, some final words burst forth. In the present day are these the United States of America or the Enslaved States of America? The United States or the Coerced States? For those paying any attention at all, these are no longer the *united* states of anything. The party has ended, but apparently nobody has gotten the memo or yet gone home. Ripe for secession, does America have any alternatives? No. The only alternatives are much more horrifying than peaceful secession. And secession stands as the only process that American institutions, protections, and ideals can today support and deliver.

Surely, many know-nothings will charge secessional speech as treasonous. Unfortunately for such simpletons, "Treason against the United States shall consist only in levying War against them, or in adhering to their Enemies, giving them Aid and Comfort" (US Constitution Article 3, Section 3). Hence, not even secession itself, let alone discussion of it, constitutes treason. Not even leaders of the Confederate States of

America were convicted of or even charged with treason after the Civil War.

US Supreme Court Justice Antonin Scalia, in his dissent from the Arizona immigration decision in 2012, bluntly stated that if the states had known the degree to which presidential powers (those exercised by Obama and approved by the Court's majority) would expand, the states never would have joined the Union in the first place. This undigested but judicially reasonable salvo must become a rallying cry for Red States exiting what has become nothing but an oppressive union. Yes, states long ago joined a union, but that union has gone voluntarily and irretrievably amok. No argument that the states must now idly suffer can ultimately prevail. Around the world and across her own chronology, America has always stood against such dictatorial stances. How can she now apply lesser standards to herself?

America remains one of the few remaining havens giving any heed to the ideals and protections of speech. In that, America must weather expressions of ideas, particularly those ideas far superior to those espoused by current officeholders. Even when speech broaches topics other than Blue favorites of gay rights or the vacuuming of fetuses, America must restrain any insecure tendencies to silence dissidents. Unless secession's opponents argue that secessional talk amounts to aiding and abetting an enemy of the state, then speech rights allow the conversation to proceed unhindered. Conveniently labeling residents of Kansas as enemies in order to quell secessional conversation will not fly. Equating residents of Oklahoma with al-Qaeda in order to dampen talk of secession will also not work. Obama, the Blues, the undecided, the bleating pundits, and the mindless media must engage secession on its merits.

Reds do not have a jealously terroristic or treasonous goal such as the destruction of others, but only a noble, self-determining aim to restore sensibility, governance, and livelihoods. Blues will holler "treason" and many other ignorant slogans not because the labels apply, but because Blues will grasp at anything to stop their meal tickets, their blood banks, their money supplies, and their overly patient tag-along Reds from getting away once and for all. So, prepare for red-herring kitchen sinks to come flying across discussion boards and dinner tables, but pay them no never-mind!

From the unanimous Declaration of the thirteen states 236 years ago, America's originators agreed:

> "When in the Course of human events, it becomes necessary for one people to dissolve the political bands which have connected them with another, and to assume among the powers of the Earth, the separate and equal station to which the Laws of Nature and of Nature's God entitle them, a decent respect to the opinions of mankind requires that they should declare the causes which impel them to the separation."

A similar such course of human events abuts American life today. The "Laws of Nature" and "Nature's God" remain unchangingly loyal to people at individual levels first and foremost. While the compelling causes for separation are but touched upon in this work, Reds must press them in peaceful discourse and civil action going forward. But in no case shall the Reds expend any more energy arguing with the Blues. The time for peaceful dissolution has come.

The 13th Amendment, the fruit of the Civil War, provides that "Neither slavery nor involuntary servitude, except as a punishment for crime whereof the party shall have been duly convicted, shall exist within the United States, or any place subject to their jurisdiction." That 1865 protection was essentially gutted by the 16th amendment authorizing income tax collections starting in 1913, which has effectuated forms of involuntary servitude against those who dare to earn a living or be otherwise financially responsible or free. For 100 years, Americans have obediently paid the increasing tax freight of this 16th Amendment. But now, with the scheme having gone predictably awry, the murmurs and din of a people's uprising can be heard. If only the first Civil War's emancipations had been left alone.

Today, peaceful and intelligible protestations have fallen on deaf ears just as in 1776 when it was said in the Declaration that "Our repeated Petitions have been answered only by repeated injury" and that "A Prince whose character is thus marked by every act which may define a Tyrant, is unfit to be the ruler of a free people." History, sensibility, rightness, and God in Heaven all weigh heavily against the status quo of 2013. America's present parallels the pre-Revolutionary climate more with each passing day. Perhaps the powers that be assume that the once rabble-rousing republic has finally and permanently been sedated into an obedient democracy.

Time is of the essence. Freedom and free people cannot wait any longer. Secessional gears must start rotating and grinding immediately during this 2012-election hangover. Seriously, who in the world would or should further tolerate the emaciation and emasculation of America? Liberty-loving people have always spoken, acted, and mobilized against this type of voluntary decay. Unless Americans have been hypnotized into dozing like the rest of the average world, this diseased government shall be divorced soon.

President Obama had his chance, but he has miserably failed to utter or do anything indicating any capacity to grasp the magnitude and depth of the troubles staring down the country. He clearly has nothing relevant to say. And though his rabid supporters cheer his do-nothing regime, free and realistic people must opt out of this next round of vacant leadership. Whereas Obama may see the Red States as hemmed in, unable to cobble together his electoral or popular defeat, he and the Republicans as well seem blind to the secessional option that must soon be exercised by the living.

With Obama's 2012 win, Red States, not just individual petitioners, must begin drafting and tendering their articles of secession. In that, they will join and promote an entirely new process and paradigmatic shift to serve notice to the nation, to the world, and to their soon-to-be-citizen residents that the doors of opportunity have not been slammed shut forever but will reopen anew.

Moving On

By vote or by war, free people do not long tolerate enslavement. Unfortunately, the voting mechanism has become impotent in this excruciatingly imbecilic America. But whatever it takes, free people will be free. It is what authenticates them as free people and not just imposters or jibber-jabberers. The Red States are leaving. What is anyone really going to do about it?

Is Connecticut really going to invade Texas? On behalf of Massachusetts, will Obama really drop bombs on Alaska? Will Marines, some undoubtedly from Indiana, willingly and gladly invade and decimate the Hoosier State? In a country worn out from skirmishes in Iraq and Afghanistan, what kind of stomach remains to fight against a peaceful and exiting Tennessee?

Across the globe, America has insisted and many times intervened to keep foreign governments from turning on their own citizens. In the Obama years alone, Mubarak in Egypt, Gaddafi in Libya, and Assad in Syria were implored not to fire upon or trounce their own people. The US intervened to help depose Mubarak, now dying in prison in his eighties, and Gaddafi, killed by angry mobs in the streets. Second-guessing those destabilizing moves, the US now appeals to Assad with many words. In light of this, shall America turn its gunships and "shock and awe" upon Mississippi? If so, Obama would make Middle-Eastern despots look heavenly in comparison.

America's first Civil War, with its brutal combat, centered prominently upon the future of slavery. Today, America's second civil war would eerily and similarly concern ongoing matters of freedom and the founding rights to life, liberty, and the pursuit of happiness. The Blues have absolutely zero moral grounds upon which to oppose or fight the flight of the Reds. Only greed and continuing selfishness would prompt the Blues to do so much as protest. But, as greed and selfishness fuel the Blue agenda, America could very well end up in a new civil war disguised as something other than what it is. In this, the Blues will be shown not to be about unity or national preservation but about sucking the Reds dry in whatever ways still possible.

Free people endowed by God cannot consent to be held back in some perpetually average state. "It is for freedom that you have been set free" (Galatians 5:1). At some point, patience gives way to action, and rightfully unbound people get on with life. Undoubtedly, this remains news to those who think little of liberation. And as much as free people long to spread and offer freedom to others, such efforts cannot and shall not become to the emancipated a perpetual snare wherein willful captives refuse to seek or take their own exoduses. Free and focused, real people must eventually get on with real work. At some point, babysitting fellow adults and being endlessly opposed and drained by slow-motion politicians and other squatters fails to qualify as actual work. Reds cannot forever tolerate their own lives ebbing away in a muddle while holding out grander hopes and dreams to the perpetually dumbfounded or disinterested.

True movers and shakers cannot soar with Blue anchors strategically placed throughout the system. The Blues simply cannot and will not ever leave the people alone. They cannot help themselves. They must meddle and muddle. These represent a pair of their unfortunate life choices. It is up to unmuzzled people to extricate themselves from the Blues. Unbecoming both in Heaven and on Earth are free people who know better and have tasted better yet waste their time complaining about bloated Blues' heavy, annoying, over-the-shoulder hovering. The Reds must accept the sad facts, secede from the Blues, and get on with life. The Blues have not at all gotten it by now. The time will not ever come when they will get it. "Leave them, they are blind guides!" Jesus conceded in Matthew 15:14. No more suffocating oppression can be afforded by anyone, anymore. Enough already.

Many Americans may feel a disturbing disloyalty in joining or supporting Red-State secession. After all, patriots have fought for America and long for national unity and pride. How could such citizens now allow, support, or precipitate the disintegration of the United States?

Actually, all must already acknowledge that America is simply no longer America. Captive to fear, betrayed by history's most corrupt government, willfully invaded by illegal immigrants whom it now sets out to legitimize, duped into frittering away history's greatest wealth and exchanging it for history's greatest debt, and suffocating beneath an electorate joyfully voting its instinctive, unreasoning self-interest, America has already slipped away, deep into a brain-damaged coma. All observant attending physicians would recommend pulling the plug to let her go. She would not want to live like this: impotent, dopey, and shameful. Long after her founding glory and burgeoning youth, America peaked with Reagan but has nosedived with Obama. Nobody coddles corpses. Hugging and kissing America as if she were coming back to life is only the crazed work of the distraught. Bury her. Honor her by re-launching her in a refreshed, remnant form. America has often been called an idea, not a place. How true. The fuller ideas and ideals of America shall re-emerge in her Red States, where freedom shall mean something once again.

Perhaps one day, long from now, after the Blues have tasted the price of themselves, a reunification of America stands as a slight but guarded possibility. Aboard a restored constitution free of devastating activist judicial opinions, perhaps America could be America again. No longer a welfare state propagated by an incorrigibly half-witted population, America could make it if her unique protections were granted to people who love freedom rather than wasted on people who love things. Limits to this reunion scenario will directly track Blue inability to learn or to see the light. No limits reside in the hearts or minds of Reds, who for love of God, love of country, and love of all have been forced to leave town.

Man has a duty not to waste. The constant stalemates and gridlock can never effect deliverance for America. Year-round campaign modes only further distract and delay. Red States will either turn the page and dawn a new day, or America will come apart limb from limb. The ridiculous tug of war between Blue and Red must come to an abrupt halt. Cloture lies with Reds because hardened Blues live upon and live for such unfruitful wrangling. The Reds must pull out. It will happen no other way. Strikingly, the back-and-forth produces nothing at all, ever. Could anyone possibly need any more evidence? The perpetual uncertainty, last-minute governing, and endless tactical gamesmanship run the responsible ragged, and all for the pointlessly cheap thrills of know-nothings and do-nothings.

Across a new landscape featuring real choices and a variety of sovereign nations, Americans would most likely reside initially wherever they wished. Waste and wrestling would end. Promise and possibility would gleam. No more enmity need persist. Voluntarily and wisely, new alliances would be formed and/or reformed.

The original Tea Party in Boston signified that colonists were finally fed up enough with Britain that they would no longer tolerate the Crown's nonsense. This exactly parallels the case for the Red States in America in 2013. CNBC's Rick Santelli struck a deeply agitated chord in 2009 when he suggested that he would organize a tea party near Lake Michigan to protest the backward economic policies of the Obama Administration, which continued to reward bad behavior and penalize good behavior. Santelli's rant riled many into action, spawned the Tea Party movement, and created political waves that one year later deposed Nancy Pelosi's House Speakership, eliminated President Obama's Congressional supermajority and simple majority, and gave indication that the country might undergo a political reversal to right and salvage America. However, the overall and continuing results have been mixed. The country has sunken substantially deeper into debt and despair, and Tea Party enthusiasm has waned as the demographics put mathematical writing on the wall that what must be done cannot be accomplished through popular vote elections across the United States. So, secession—not rallies, gatherings, or ballot efforts—will measure the will and the impact of the Tea Party sequel just as it marked its predecessor. The Boston original, the one Santelli suggested repeating, which was not a political movement but a breakaway from tyranny, remains a vitally essential vehicle through which Reds shall announce and symbolize the return of individual autonomy to Americans. This act will result in secession of Red States—the only remaining hope for American ideas and ideals.

The people, led by authentic proponents of freedom, must begin making their moves over the next few years. As usual, Americans have waited patiently, verifying failure of all options before setting out to act on a grand scale. But now, with time and options withering, gears of secession must begin to rotate in uncompromising and unstoppable ways. Surely, nothing associated with the irrational musings already insufferably tolerated can be entertained any further.

Final Clearance

So could it really be? Must America break apart? Is this really the end? Yep. A final check of systems shows no other way. During Obama's early White House years, this writer reached some conclusions and verbally proffered secession as America's only option going forward. Since Obama's re-election, individuals in every state have filed secession petitions with the White House. This yet preliminary gesture portends a forthcoming narrative seeking release of the captives, whereby Moses and Jesus stand as chronological and unerring forbearers.

Very unlike Moses and Jesus, however, several outspoken GOP governors' predictably poured cold water on the secessional petitions. Texas' Rick Perry said through a spokesperson that he did not support them, Louisiana's Bobby Jindal labeled secession "silly," and South Carolina's Nikki Haley pooh-poohed the idea as having been tried before. These reactions, while annoyingly politically correct, again demonstrate how the Republican Party remains a substantial part of the problem. Appeasing the public and foolishly eyeing 2016 as another crack at the already rotten apple, these governors disown their very lips, which had previously spoken of grander, more honorable, and more invigorating ideals. They and their ilk show a perpetual unwillingness to add their lives, fortunes, and sacred honors to the cause as the Founders had so commendably committed in the Declaration.

Though petitions for secession have already been delivered to the president, let everyone be clear that true emancipation comes from God and not by way of anybody else. Accustomed to begging governments for green lights, Americans must shake themselves and cleanse themselves of both dust and rust. Freedom remains a God-given right, not a political gift or wish-list item.

Still gluttonous for disappointment, many so-called "conservatives" express hope and optimism that Florida Senator Marco Rubio will run for president in 2016, garner enough Hispanic votes due to his Cuban pedigree, and regain the White House for the GOP. These wishful thinkers have become so bewildered and desperate that they have willfully forgotten the mighty tumble that has befallen America. At the beginning, free men and women could make a go of it and through hard work and individual ambition make anything happen. Now, less than 250 years later, this same ambitious lot has been reduced to hoping that, well down the road, a like-kind candidate might be able to convince a rising tide of immigrants to allow free people to live and be, well, free! Since when has the American ideal of freedom granted from Heaven been downgraded to a freedom conferred by voting blocs lured by way of candidates' external appearances? What god would honor such a demented and diminished hope or plan? Surely not the God in Heaven. So a Rubio win might be great for America, especially if he holds firm to Red ideology, but nobody's victory can, should, or will determine whether free people can be free or not.

True patriots must emerge, forsaking the lukewarm and gaining Heaven's favor for another shot at life that can truly be considered life. The overwhelmed, the undecided, and the reluctant will follow later. True believers must step uncompromisingly to the fore. The discussion going forward must unapologetically concern only the timing and the logistics of secession, and not the machinations or options of business-as-usual politics.

Seceding Red States shall first brandish their decisions to secede. Via legislatures and governors, or by way of ballot referenda, seceding states must announce their appropriate declarations. Second, the US Supreme Court will decide upon any federal objections. That case and ruling will not bind the seceding states but may bind feds from intervening. Thus it is in the best interest of Red States to proceed with this step. Third, seceding Red States shall undertake and effectuate what they have in mind to do. They shall amend their state constitutions to avoid going Blue once Blues migrate to Red States for opportunity and economy. Fourth and last, Red States must impress upon the feds that remaining in the old Union is not an option. Seceding Red States hold all of the cards here. The feds will not bomb seceding states. The feds cannot even manage a completely compliant people. The last thing the feds want or need is a tussle with awakened Reds. The Reds must know and remember this and pay no attention to the federal and Blue objections which contain no sound rationale but only predictable blustering.

The matter of "who is right?" and "who is wrong?" will be settled the old-fashioned way: by empirical proof. Seceded Red States will demonstrably leave remaining Blue States in the proverbial dust. The zeal, renewal, limitlessness, economic activity, and ingenuity in favor of Red Nations will sharply and manifestly contrast with the tired, communal, rationed, tightened lives in the Blue States. No question will remain for anyone with eyes and ears. The Red Nations will have become the New America.

The same itty-bitty people who brought America to her knees beneath $16 trillion in debt will, unable to contain their silliness, proffer many arguments against secession. Those inclined to give them an ear should do the world a favor and stay with the Blues. Red-Nation emergence will never find itself desperate for the compromised, the political, or the doubtful. Anyone still able to listen to the Blues should go the rest of the way and join the Blues. Now is not the time for compromise. Now is the time to join one side or the other. Those in the middle shall be counted as de facto Blues until they learn enough to see the light and take a real stand. The Red Nations will not be desperate. They will be leaving desperation behind.

Secession shall begin the long-awaited reshuffling of the middle of the continent. The unacquainted, culturally adrift, and convulsively immoral will no longer roadblock the autonomies and callings of others. Let this be the end or the beginning. Whichever, it cannot any longer be as it is.

The motto of the conflicted Blue State of New Hampshire, "Live Free or Die," must now become the valiant and unrelenting mantra of seceding Red States. Though severely outnumbered on the planet, there still exist some people who agree with the spirit of America's founding. Quotes, slogans, principles, founding verbiage, and other pronouncements of free people declaring and re-possessing their God-given rights still ring true in those for whom liberation actually matters. To the rest, they need not trouble themselves trying to wrap their minds or hearts around it. They will have no trouble finding predators to exploit them, lie to them, and expend them even as they breathe.

However, for those for whom freedom is like oxygen, the game is over, the country has ended, and emancipation by secession must be at hand. Either by peaceful divorce with Blue States or by world-ending Civil War II, the Red States are leaving the monstrosity of Obama's nation. The Blues do not understand this, and the time for explaining it has run out. C'est la vie.

Prerequisite to the newly free part of the old America, happiness must be understood. Blues grab money, give it away, and in horror cannot figure out why happiness has not multiplied. Blues do not understand that love of money remains a well-known source of all kinds of evil and that money does not generate happiness. Rather, camaraderie, peace of mind, working hard with hands, open weeknights and weekends, undisturbed time with loved ones, an early retirement, and many other money-neutral intangibles facilitate happiness and fulfillment. Common skills, hometown allegiances, and even the bonds of union brotherhood can provide the spice of life to many without any infusion of money, let alone someone else's money.

In a truly free society, the Declaration's "pursuit of happiness" reasserts itself as a highly valued and fiercely protected right. In America's present situation, the pursuit is throttled through an obstacle course, a horror house, and a meat grinder before it ever returns to its rightful owner. Red-State departures will return first principles to a people no longer settling for phony lives devoid of such principles. All systems show secession to be a "go."

Lift-off

What will secession's results look like? Ultimately, a slice of heaven, no doubt. Red States will first secede and then, amid an agreeable calm and an exhilarating air, shall regroup and set upon ambitious and fitting courses filled with possibilities. With ad nauseam argumentation relegated to a painfully Blue thing of the past, citizens of seceding Red States shall immediately get to work on things that matter. Over time, Reds will show the world that citizenries containing equal parts liberty and responsibility underpin the strongest, most prosperous, and most attractive places on Earth. Americans envisioned exactly this at the beginning and modeled it across much of the nation's history. Sadly, however, a pathetic and rising tide of loosening standards and the election of cold and abominable leadership arose to shutter freedoms, stifle ambitions, and extricate from the people notions of responsibility, which would in time cost the very liberty upon which America was founded.

Red States' constitutional requirements for balanced budgets shall be retained on the front end, bolstered over time, and offered to the world to demonstrate how government business ought to be conducted. Each seceding state shall receive a credit rating contemplative of its own sovereign and fiscal standing. This will trigger the beginnings of the great economic divide between seceding Red States and abandoned Blue States. New Red nations will gain favorable credit terms, will encourage business and industry, and will be at liberty to floor their gas pedals economically. Open and free markets, rewarded entrepreneurship, a simple and fair tax code, long-term planning on the basis of transparent and reliable governance, a convergence of occupations and workers, and the reemergence of independence and charity will nearly immediately catapult seceding Red States into an economic stratosphere. Given these wonderful prospects for emancipated people, citizens of Red nations shall never again tolerate the debilitating waywardness that drove America's decline and collapse: giveaways to some and the emergence of a political class built upon such a meritless system.

Red Nations will establish their own currencies, readily and transparently trading them upon world markets, and they shall be well served to avoid quagmires like the Euro currency. No longer financially drained by Washington and no longer having to play "cat and mouse" to retrieve monies usurped by federal overlords, Red States shall find themselves once again limited only by the distant bounds of ingenuity. They will manage their own borders and enter cooperative agreements with other nations. In any case, the choking restrictor plates placed on former Red States will be removed, and flight and every other ambition shall become possible once again.

On national defense, Red Nations will enthusiastically and innovatively configure strategies, logistics, and alliances. They would each likely develop and maintain nuclear defense and declare to the world that they are not to be messed with. A full, destructive response to terrorists will very likely replace the timid policies of conventional, protracted, and bankrupting wars.

Red Nations will decide the extent to which they will protect their domestic industries and thereby encourage provision of middle-class employment. Therefore, they will make do without the cheap lures and simple solutions dangled by Wal-Mart, the Chinese, and the welfare state. In addition, Red Nations will assume their per capita share of the American national debt. They will repay their creditors directly, leaving the witless Blue States as singular defaulters due to their lack of an actual economy. In about zero seconds, the Red Nations will become the envy of the world and of the worn-out and farcical Blue version of America.

Safeguards

Seceding Red States must enjoy all-new choices along with their own new countries, destinies, dreams, and paths. In their new constitutions, Red States must make certain that the meat hooks of the Blues can never regain even a hint of their historical clutches. Like moss, algae, and noxious gases, the meat-hook hungers of the Blues will work overtly, covertly, and tirelessly to grab hold of the Reds yet again. The Blues seriously have nothing else to do other than to trouble and bother the Reds. This must not be tolerated any longer for God may not much longer tolerate those Reds who know better and yet willingly fail to do better.

States must make clean breaks from the US and from other states, or they will be subject to wrestling, arguing, grappling, and muddling to the middle forever. Blue doctrine is a disease that spreads and kills. Only those already given over to it and given up for it seem immune and blasé about it all. Without a clean break and a new, solid, and hardly amendable constitution, even seceded Red States will succumb to the age-old toleration of idea exchanges with idiots, resulting in curses from Heaven for being so ludicrous. Without a healthy disdain for all things Blue, Red-State emancipation will never last or matter.

Had America's founders lived forever, their guiding narratives and arguments would likely have staved off the country's dismantling. Somehow, Red States must enact constitutions that cannot be changed by wimpy, "wiser" future generations that only plant seeds of destruction without regard to or respect of what had been carefully crafted at the inception of a braver new world. As with New Mexico and Nevada already, and Arizona and Texas in the near future, newly emancipated Red States will be invaded by new "citizen" voters seeking the best prospects on the continent and ironically and irrationally predisposed to turning things Blue. This always happens, since Blues move to Red territories because Red locales always produce much superior financial, environmental, and upwardly mobilizing oases. Amazingly, Blues do not give thought to their ways, as they then ruin Red regions by turning them pink, purple, and then ultimately Blue at the polls. Smart, savvy, and strong prohibitions against these erosions must be made. Ronald Reagan famously spoke at the Republican National Convention in 1964, saying that the United States represented freedom's last chance on Earth. Now, only the seceding Red States represent freedom's last chance. Thus, those leading such new nations and those crafting and approving their new documents must vigorously protect inter-generational individuals from the emergence and growth of a bloated welfare state in ways so far inadequately curbed in the United States. Impotent vision and soft leadership need never apply for this crucial task. Such a courageous Red course calls for the selflessly ambitious to lead and persuade others of mankind's true calling.

Accordingly, laws and safeguards must be enacted to manage migrations from Blue States to Red States. In short order, economies in Blue States will crumble to the ground, and there will be much predictable yet long-avoidable bawling. The Blues will then do what they always do: look to the Reds for rescue. As is painfully obvious by now, the Blues cannot help themselves. This is how they are. Gone should be the notion that Blues can be talked to, reasoned with, won over, or made reflective. They are forever disposed to their own self-destruction and to the demolition of those amenable to the latch of their words and ways. If Reds are not prepared to deal with these philosophical and political realities, then they might as well stay in the Union and succumb sooner rather than later!

Red Nations must enact new and durable constitutions of their choosing. They must enact true immigration policies and constitutional dictates. They should anticipate a migratory flood of Blue-State residents seeking opportunities in Red Nations. They must take steps to prevent the illegal-alien invasion America suffered in her latter years. They must also beware any hint of immigration that reverses the freedoms upon which the Red Nations were founded. With disparate birthrates across demographics, Red Nations must beware even legal immigration slowly transforming them into Blue Nations in the same way America succumbed to Blueness even after its legendary and landmarked start.

"Any kingdom divided against itself will be ruined, and a house divided against itself will fall" (Luke 11:17). Surely, America's now-permanent divisions are only deepening and widening. She cannot and will not stand. Reds must either castrate themselves and their ideals in order to tolerate and live with the Blues or secede and build newly unified kingdoms and houses that will stand and lead the world into free, smart, and prosperous tomorrows.

Conversational Starting Point

Rightly received, this national scolding will swiftly give rise to more than a thousand freshly modern topics of conversation. Selfless grown-ups will press back firmly and unapologetically against the ever-simmering whine of hopelessly miserly adults. A new day will dawn and a renewed world will unfold. Limitless potentials will once again come available for all of those housing genuine concern for others in their hearts, minds, and souls.

For conversational starters, freed men and women must expose the basis of America's great divide: the fact that while rights and sovereignties mean little or nothing to most, there still remain those for whom such divinely distributed privileges mean more than life itself. Truly, therein lies today's rub between Blue and Red in America. Confronting Blues' lack of proper regard for individual liberty will begin to uncover the real issues presently killing the country and wasting precious lives and opportunities. By addressing these roots and no longer playing dumb, Reds will overtake and drive America's forthcoming conversations, choices and pathways.

ABOUT THE AUTHOR

Evangelist, educator, and esquire, Trent W. Ling resides in Orlando, Florida. Contact information and bona fides remain readily available at www.TrentLing.com. Further information specifically relevant to this work can be heard at the audio links www.TrentLing.com/audio-dead-in-the-water and www.TrentLing.com/podcast-i-dont-care-i-love-you.

REFERENCES

International Bible Society (1984). The Holy Bible, New International Version. Grand Rapids, Michigan: Zondervan.

The United States Constitution and Related Documents (2007). Melville, New York: Graphic Image, Inc.

www.ingramcontent.com/pod-product-compliance
Lightning Source LLC
Chambersburg PA
CBHW022115280326
41933CB00007B/396
9780615682464